Ginny Smith
101 W. River Rd. #68
Tucson, AZ 85704

P9-CWD-918

DAVID
A MAN AFTER GOD'S OWN HEART

BIBLE STUDY GUIDE

From the Bible-teaching ministry of

Charles R. Swindoll

INSIGHT FOR LIVING

Charles R. Swindoll is a graduate of Dallas Theological Seminary and has served in pastorates for more than twenty-five years, including churches in Texas, New England, and California. Since 1971 he has served as senior pastor of the First Evangelical Free Church of Fullerton, California. Chuck's radio program, "Insight for Living," began in 1979. In addition to his church and radio ministries, Chuck enjoys writing. He has authored numerous books and booklets on a variety of subjects.

Based on the outlines of Chuck's sermons, the study guide text was coauthored by Julie Martin, a graduate of Biola University and a former associate editor in the Educational Products Department at Insight for Living. The Living Insights are written by Bill Butterworth, a graduate of Florida Bible College, Dallas Theological Seminary, and Florida Atlantic University. Bill Butterworth is currently a staff writer in the Educational Products Department.

Editor in Chief:	Cynthia Swindoll
Coauthor of Text:	Julie Martin
Author of Living Insights:	Bill Butterworth
Editorial Assistant:	Glenda Schlahta
Copy Manager:	Jac La Tour
Senior Copy Editor:	Jane Gillis
Copy Editor:	Wendy Peterson
Director, Communications Division:	Carla Beck
Project Manager:	Nina Paris
Project Supervisor:	Cassandra Clark
Designer:	Steve Cox
Production Artist:	Diana Vasquez
Typographer:	Bob Haskins
Cover Photograph:	Michelangelo's *David* from Galleria dell'Accademia, Florence, Italy
Print Production Manager:	Deedee Snyder
Printer:	Frye and Smith

Unless otherwise identified, all Scripture references are from the New American Standard Bible, © The Lockman Foundation 1960, 1962, 1963, 1968, 1971, 1972, 1973, 1975, 1977. Used by permission.

© 1977, 1978, 1981, 1982, 1988 by Charles R. Swindoll. All rights reserved. Printed in the United States of America. No portion of this publication may be reproduced in any form, except for brief quotations in reviews, without prior written permission of the publisher, Insight for Living, Post Office Box 4444, Fullerton, California 92634.

ISBN 0-8499-8328-2

Ordering Information

An album that contains twenty-four messages on twelve cassettes and corresponds to this study guide may be purchased through the Sales Department of Insight for Living, Post Office Box 4444, Fullerton, California 92634. For ordering information and a current catalog, please write our office or call 1-800-772-8888.

Canadian residents may obtain a catalog and ordering information through Insight for Living Ministries, Post Office Box 2510, Vancouver, British Columbia, Canada V6B 3W7, 1-800-663-7639. Australian residents should direct their correspondence to Insight for Living Ministries, General Post Office Box 2823 EE, Melbourne, Victoria 3001. Other overseas residents should direct their correspondence to our Fullerton office.

If you wish to order by Visa or MasterCard, you are welcome to use our toll-free numbers, Monday through Friday, between the hours of 8:30 A.M. and 4:00 P.M., Pacific time. The number to call from anywhere in the United States is 1-800-772-8888. To order from Canada, call 1-800-663-7639.

Table of Contents

David . . . A Man After God's Own Heart

Few men in history have been so gifted and respected as the sweet singer of Israel, David, the youngest son of Jesse. His personality was a strange combination of simplicity and complexity. As J. Oswald Sanders wrote:

> *He swung between extremes, but paradoxically evidenced an abiding stability. The oscillating needle always returned to its pole—God Himself.**

Being a man after God's heart, David longed to serve Him well, whether as an obscure shepherd boy along the Judean hillsides or as the highest reigning monarch of authority. But woven through his enviable life were tough threads of humanity, which keep us from worshiping the man today. While great and gallant, David was nevertheless merely a man, plagued with flaws in his character and failure in his reign.

May these studies help us realize that devotion—not perfection—is the secret of living a life that pleases God. We need that reminder every day of our lives.

Chuck Swindoll

---

*J. Oswald Sanders, *Robust in Faith* (Chicago, Ill.: Moody Press, 1965), p. 117.

Putting Truth into Action

Knowledge apart from application falls short of God's desire for His children. Knowledge must result in change and growth. Consequently, we have constructed this Bible study guide with these purposes in mind: (1) to stimulate discovery, (2) to increase understanding, and (3) to encourage application.

At the end of each lesson is a section called **Living Insights.** *There you'll be given assistance in further Bible study, and you'll be encouraged to contemplate and apply the things you've learned. This is the place where the lesson is fitted with shoe leather for your walk through the varied experiences of life.*

In wrapping up some lessons, you'll find a unit called **Digging Deeper.** *It will provide you with essential information and list helpful resource materials so that you can probe further into some of the issues raised in those studies.*

It's our hope that you'll discover numerous ways to use this tool. Some useful avenues we suggest are personal meditation, joint discovery, and discussion with your spouse, family, work associates, friends, or neighbors. The study guide is also practical for Sunday school classes, Bible study groups, and, of course, as a study aid for the "Insight for Living" radio broadcast.

In order to derive the greatest benefit from this process, we suggest that you record your responses to the lessons in the space which has been provided for you. In view of the kinds of questions asked, your study guide may become a journal filled with your many discoveries and commitments. We anticipate that you will find yourself returning to it periodically for review and encouragement.

Julie Martin
Coauthor of Text

Bill Butterworth
Author of Living Insights

DAVID
A MAN AFTER
GOD'S OWN HEART

God's Heart, God's Man, God's Ways

1 Samuel 13:13–14, 16:1; Psalm 78:70–72

David.

Jesse's youngest son. Youthful shepherd of Bethlehem. Giant-slayer. Teen-aged king-elect. Composer of psalms. Saul's personal musician. Jonathan's closest friend.

He rose from hunted fugitive to Israel's king. And he fell from champion in battle to aged and troubled monarch.

David—a man of glorious triumph, yet great tragedy. Uniquely gifted, but human to the core; strong in battle, but weak at home. Why are we drawn to study his life? Because David isn't a polished-marble personality. He is blood and bone and breath, sharing our struggles of spirit and soul.

Before delving into the events that sculpted the life of David—the man after God's own heart—we'll take some time to look at what's important to God's heart and how that led to David's anointing.

I. A Principle Worth Remembering

Since David was the only person in all Scripture whose epitaph reads "man after God's own heart," we might think of him as some kind of spiritual Superman in a world without a trace of kryptonite. But he wasn't studded with superhuman qualities. God doesn't select His servants on the basis of Atlas physiques or Einstein intellects. As Paul told the believers at Corinth:

> For consider your calling, brethren, that there were not many wise according to the flesh, not many mighty, not many noble; but God has chosen the foolish things of the world to shame the wise, and God has chosen the weak things of the world to shame the things which are strong, and the base things of the world and the despised, God has chosen, the things that are not, that He might nullify the things that are, that no man should boast before God. (1 Cor. 1:26–29)

1

This New Testament passage echoes the Old Testament truth that resounds throughout the life of David: *God's method of choosing servants runs contrary to human reason.* That a young shepherd boy would be anointed Israel's next king made no sense in the world's mind. But in the mind of God, impressed not by brawn or brains but by a heart completely His, it made perfect sense.

II. The Jews' Historical Backdrop

Like the difference in taste between a twist of lemon and a drop of honey, man's way and God's way of selecting leaders stand in sharp contrast. God's way was shown in the often sweet reign of David. And man's way, in the bitter reign of Saul.

A. The people's choice. From Eden's forbidden fruit to twentieth-century democracy, "the people's choice" has always been a podium for self-centered demands. Let's take a look at how Israel's choice became her curse.

1. **Their times.** Forty years before David's inauguration, the period of the judges came to an end. Lethargy, apathy, compromise, and selfishness had swamped the Israelite camp. Eli, the venerable high priest, was long since dead. And the one bright light on the horizon, Samuel, had eyes that were dimming: he was growing old. Normally, the leadership would have been passed down to Samuel's sons, however,

> [they] did not walk in his ways, but turned aside after dishonest gain and took bribes and perverted justice. (8:3)

The Israelites were on a long drift from their God.

2. **Their demand.** Dissatisfied and disillusioned, the Israelites wanted a king. So they approached Samuel at Ramah, saying:

> "Behold, you have grown old, and your sons do not walk in your ways. Now appoint a king for us to judge us like all the nations." (v. 5)

They wanted to be "like all the nations." What they had forgotten is that the other nations were headed for hell.

3. **Samuel's response.** The Israelites' demand pinned and needled Samuel's heart.

> But the thing was displeasing in the sight of Samuel when they said, "Give us a king to judge us." (v. 6a)

No doubt feeling rejected, Samuel fell to his knees in prayer. The Lord's answer salved his sense of failure and granted the Israelites' demand.

> And the Lord said to Samuel, "Listen to the voice of the people in regard to all that they say to you, for they have not rejected you, but they have

rejected Me from being king over them. . . . Now then, listen to their voice; however, you shall solemnly warn them and tell them of the procedure of the king who will reign over them." (vv. 7, 9)

They would have their wish, but at the high cost of their freedom. And as the Lord predicted (see vv. 11–18), they ended up sorry they ever mentioned the word *king*.

4. **Saul chosen.** If Israel had been a car lot, Saul would have been Cadillac's classiest model, loaded with all the extras—he was the tallest, most handsome man among them (see 9:2). Yes, Saul looked good in the Israelites' eyes. But his height and good looks couldn't hide his small and homely heart, which showed itself in selfishness, egotism, paranoia, depression, and violence.

B. The Lord's choice. As the marks of weak character began to scar Saul's life, God began to look for a replacement. This time it would be *His* choice—a choice based not on human reason, but on three essential qualifications of the heart.

1. **Spirituality.** God looks for those with hearts like His own. As Samuel told Saul:

> "But now your kingdom shall not endure. The Lord has sought out for Himself a man after His own heart, and the Lord has appointed him as ruler over His people, because you have not kept what the Lord commanded you." (13:14)

Being a person after God's own heart means living in harmony with Him; being burdened by His burdens; obeying His command to go to the right, to the left, or to stay right where you are. In a nutshell, it's having a heart that's completely His.

> "For the eyes of the Lord move to and fro throughout the earth that He may strongly support those whose heart is completely His." (2 Chron. 16:9a)

Completely His

When God's searching eyes stop and fix their gaze on *you,* does He find a heart fully committed to Him? A heart grieved by wrong, intent on avoiding what displeases Him?

Does He find a heart *completely* His?

---

2. **Humility.** As 2 Chronicles 16:9a tells us, God seeks those with committed hearts that He might support them, because His choice is the one who is teachable, humble, dependent,

and reliant on Himself. Mighty Saul, the people's choice, failed. But David, God's humble servant, was upheld by His hand. Servants are those who are genuinely unaware of themselves—completely unconcerned about who gets the glory, what image they're projecting, or what people might say about them. The seeds of a servant's heart grow best in the fertile soil of humility.

3. **Integrity.** David's heart was wholesome and pure. He measured his life with the unbending yardstick of integrity.

> He also chose David His servant,
> And took him from the sheepfolds;
> From the care of the ewes with suckling lambs
> He brought him,
> To shepherd Jacob His people,
> And Israel His inheritance.
> So he shepherded them *according to the integrity[1] of his heart,*
> And guided them with his skillful hands.
> (Ps. 78:70–72, emphasis added)

God has little use for handsome, charismatic Sauls. What He values most are deeply spiritual, genuinely humble, honest-to-the-core servants. And He found these qualities in the character of the young shepherd boy David.

The Acid Test

"No, God does not see as man sees. He does not measure character by charisma. He does not defer to human values. God's chief criterion for selecting special servants for mighty purposes is: *'Are you willing to do My will?'* This is the acid test. Despite all of an individual's other failings, if above all else his one consuming desire is to be *'a man after God's own heart (will),'* he will be lifted above the turmoil of his times, in great honor."[2]

III. The Lord's Method of Training

Before David was lifted to his place of honor on the throne of Israel, God had been training him. Not in the pompous schools of royalty, but right where he was.

---

1. In Hebrew, the word *integrity* means "completeness, wholeness, innocence, simplicity of life, sound, unimpaired."

2. W. Phillip Keller, *David: The Time of Saul's Tyranny* (Waco, Tex.: Word Books, 1985), vol. 1, p. 76.

A. Solitude. When you live in the fields, tending sheep, it is solitude that nurtures you. F. B. Meyer writes:

> Nature was his nurse, his companion, his teacher.... The moorlands around Bethlehem, forming the greater part of the Judaean plateau do not, however, present features of soft beauty; but are wild, gaunt, strong—character-breeding. There shepherds have always led and watched their flocks; and there David first imbibed that knowledge of natural scenery and of pastoral pursuits which coloured all his after life and poetry, as the contents of the vat the dyer's hand. Such were the schools and schoolmasters of his youth.[3]

B. Obscurity. David's character wasn't built by the marbled columns of pride. It was built by the clay and straw bricks of faithfulness in the little things—the unseen, unknown, unappreciated, and unapplauded.

C. Monotony. God allowed David to wrestle with insignificance and routine. And with no relief in sight, David carried on—faithfully, daily.

D. Reality. Solitude...obscurity...monotony. No, God didn't train David to be some sort of irresponsible mystic who sits on top of a hill, pops birdseed, whistles Sunday-school choruses—and when he gets a sudden wave of energy, teaches the sheep to roll over. David's training exposed him to the dangers and threats of reality (see 1 Sam. 17:33–37). While David was tending his sheep—in solitude and obscurity—God put steel in his bones. When faced with fighting all 9½ feet of Goliath's iron body, David told Saul with bold assurance,

> "The Lord who delivered me from the paw of the lion and from the paw of the bear, He will deliver me from the hand of this Philistine." (v. 37a)

IV. Two Important Truths

Notice that David didn't prove his character in that one-time battle with Goliath, but day in and day out in the fields, with the lion and the bear. Before we close, let's home in on two truths we can take with *us* to the fields, where we live our lives.

A. It's in the little things that we prove ourselves capable of the big things. Before entrusting David with the lives of the entire nation of Israel, God first gave him a flock of sheep to protect (compare Matt. 25:14–30, especially vv. 21, 23).

B. When God develops inner qualities, He's never in a hurry. Although souls are saved in a mere moment, character

3. F. B. Meyer, *David* (Grand Rapids, Mich.: Zondervan Publishing House, 1953), pp. 12–13.

is developed only with time. Giving us time to grow is part of His plan of grace (see Phil. 1:6). Just remember that no matter how much growth you have yet to do, no matter how out of place you might feel as His servant, you are—like David—God's choice.

Set among Princes

"Remember, dear friend, that it matters not what your occupation may be, you may yet have the privilege of the kingdom. David was but a shepherd and yet he was raised to the throne, and so shall each believer be. You may be obscure and unknown, in your father's house the very least, and yet you may share a filial part in the divine heart. You may be among those who never would be mentioned except as mere units of the general census, without parts, without position; you may almost think yourself to have less than the one talent; you may conceive yourself to be a worm and no man, and like David you may say, 'I was as a beast before Thee'; and yet think of this, that the marvellous election of God can stoop from the highest throne of glory to lift the beggar from the dunghill and set him among princes."[4]

 Living Insights

Study One

David—living proof that God's choice of servants runs contrary to human reason.

- First Corinthians 1:26–29 outlines the qualities God looks for. Let's probe into this text. Use a Bible concordance or a dictionary to discover the meanings behind the key words and phrases that follow.

1 Corinthians 1:26–29

Wise according to the flesh: _____

_____

_____

_____

---

4. Charles Haddon Spurgeon, *The Treasury of the Bible* (Grand Rapids, Mich.: Zondervan Publishing House, 1968), vol. 1, p. 655.

Mighty: _____

_____

_____

_____

Noble: _____

_____

_____

_____

Foolish: _____

_____

_____

_____

Weak: _____

_____

_____

_____

Base: _____

_____

_____

_____

Despised: _____

_____

_____

_____

No man should boast before God: _____

_____

_____

_____

Continued on next page

Living Insights

In God's set of scales, appearances don't weigh much. What does weigh heavily in His mind is our hearts.

● Three qualities that matter deeply to God are spirituality, humility, and integrity. How are you developing in these three areas? Which ones need the most work? Take a few minutes to write out your thoughts and feelings, and make some plans for improvement.

Spirituality

_____

_____

_____

_____

_____

Humility

_____

_____

_____

_____

_____

Integrity

_____

_____

_____

_____

_____

A Nobody, Nobody Noticed
1 Samuel 16:1–13

The year 1809 was a very good year.

Of course, nobody knew it at the time, because every eye was on Napoleon, as he swept across Austria like a frenzied flame in a parched wheat field. Little else seemed significant; the diminutive dictator of France was the talk of all Europe. The terror of his reign made his name a synonym for military superiority and ruthless ambition.

That same year, while war was being waged and history was being made, babies were being born in England and America. But who had time to think about babies and bottles and cradles and cribs when Austria was falling?

Somebody should have.

In 1809, a veritable host of thinkers and statesmen drew their first breaths. William Gladstone was born in Liverpool. Alfred Tennyson began his life in Lincolnshire. Oliver Wendell Holmes made his first cry in Cambridge, Massachusetts. Edgar Allan Poe, in nearby Boston, began his poignant life. And in Hodgenville, Kentucky, in a rugged log cabin owned by an illiterate laborer and his wife, were heard the tiny screams of their newborn son, Abraham Lincoln.

All this and more happened in 1809. But nobody noticed. The destiny of the world was being shaped by Napoleon over in Austria. Or was it? The "nobodies" nobody noticed were, in fact, the genesis of a new era. It was their lives, their brains, their writings that would dent the destiny of the entire world.

The year 1020 B.C. was also a very good year.

But not because of Saul, the Napoleon of that day. Saul, Israel's elected king, had begun to fissure under the weighty demands of his role. Rashness, compromise, rationalization, and open disobedience to God soon began to seep into the cracks and saturate his shattered character with sin. Until, finally, Samuel confronted him, telling him that God had rejected him as Israel's king (1 Sam. 15:23, 26).

That year was especially significant because, while everyone was watching Saul's reign sink, in a secluded field in Bethlehem God was raising up a youth named David—a nobody who would change Israel's course forever.

I. Man Panics, God Provides
All eyes had been on Saul. Now, suddenly, he was stripped of his authority; God had rejected him as Israel's king.

A. Saul's failure. Most likely, the news of Samuel's confrontation with Saul (1 Sam. 15:12–35) started a national panic. Although the nation was worse off because of Saul's reign, the people felt they would be lost without a king. To them, no king meant no protection, and defeat seemed inevitable. They had forgotten that God was their ultimate protector, their shield and sword— that at that very moment He'd already chosen the right man to replace Saul.

B. Samuel's fear. We would think that Samuel, God's spokesman, would have remembered that God is always at work behind the scenes—that he wouldn't have feared for his future. But the prophet is human enough to tremble in his sandals at the thought of crossing the king. But God reassures Samuel:

> "How long will you grieve over Saul, since I have rejected him from being king over Israel? Fill your horn with oil, and go; I will send you to Jesse the Bethlehemite, for I have selected a king for Myself among his sons." But Samuel said, "How can I go? When Saul hears of it, he will kill me." And the Lord said, "Take a heifer with you, and say, 'I have come to sacrifice to the Lord.' And you shall invite Jesse to the sacrifice, and I will show you what you shall do; and you shall anoint for Me the one whom I designate to you." (16:1–3)

What Tomorrow Holds

Like Samuel, are you unsure of what tomorrow holds? Uncertain about the end of this week? Are you wondering where your business is leading you, or whether or not to make a career change? The comforting thing is that God knows. And He will lead you if you'll wait ... and listen ... and rest in Him.

While we panic, He is already quietly moving behind the scenes. Before we call, He is answering. And when we are uncertain, He is calm—sure of what tomorrow holds. We may not know what tomorrow holds ... but we know *who* holds tomorrow!

II. Man Looks, God Sees

Samuel doesn't hesitate to obey God's instructions.

> So Samuel did what the Lord said, and came to Bethlehem. And the elders of the city came trembling to meet him and said, "Do you come in peace?" (v. 4)

Samuel's arrival was no small matter to the people of Bethlehem. No doubt, word of his visit had rippled through the city's streets, and the people were afraid—much like we might be if the head of the CIA or FBI dropped by for a chat. But Samuel assures them of his peaceful intentions, and he calls together Jesse and his sons to participate in a sacrifice (v. 5), during which the prophet will scout out God's chosen man. The first to catch Samuel's eye is Eliab, son number one.

> Then it came about when they entered, that he looked at Eliab and thought, "Surely the Lord's anointed is before Him." But the Lord said to Samuel, "Do not look at his appearance or at the height of his stature, because I have rejected him; for God sees not as man sees, for man looks at the outward appearance, but the Lord looks at the heart." (vv. 6–7)

Then comes son number two.

> Then Jesse called Abinadab, and made him pass before Samuel. And he said, "Neither has the Lord chosen this one." (v. 8)

And then comes son number three.

> Next Jesse made Shammah pass by. And he said, "Neither has the Lord chosen this one." (v. 9)

And the parade continues.

> Thus Jesse made seven of his sons pass before Samuel. But Samuel said to Jesse, "The Lord has not chosen these." (v. 10)

Each of Jesse's sons *looked* like king material, but in God's book externals don't carry a lot of weight. God's choice is always based on the rock-solid qualities of the heart (v. 7b).

III. Man Forgets, God Remembers

So the seven men were seated. Apparently, these were all of Jesse's sons. However, since God had promised that the new king would be selected from among his sons, Samuel is sure there is another. A little puzzled, he asks Jesse, " 'Are these all the children?' " (v. 11a).

A. Jesse's youngest. Jesse's oh-yeah-I-almost-forgot reply reveals that David had been overlooked.

> And he said, "There remains yet the youngest, and behold, he is tending the sheep." (v. 11b)

Why wasn't David brought in with the others? Why was he left to his job in the fields when the others were being considered for a big promotion? Jesse's attitude toward David displays two mistakes parents often make.

1. He didn't appreciate each of his children equally. Jesse never intended to whistle David in from the fields.

2. He failed to cultivate a mutual respect among the brothers. Jesse's reply essentially said: "Well, yes, there's David, the youngest, but he just keeps the sheep."

Shepherds or Kings?

Parents, the greatest contribution you can make in the lives of your children, aside from introducing them to the Savior, is to help them see that they have worth and value. They need to know they have something unique to offer, just like every other member of the family.

That's where Jesse failed.

Do you communicate to your children the message that they might be the one God will choose to use in a special way? Or do you play favorites, keeping others in the fields with the sheep?

It's not in God's plan to make us all kings. But if we will robe our children with a sense of value and crown them with the jewels of self-worth, they will, when anointed by the sweet oil of the Spirit, accomplish regal things for the King.[1]

B. David's anointing. Regardless of Jesse's opinion of David, Samuel insists on seeing the young shepherd boy.

> Then Samuel said to Jesse, "Send and bring him; for we will not sit down until he comes here." So he sent and brought him in. Now he was ruddy, with beautiful eyes and a handsome appearance. And the Lord said, "Arise, anoint him; for this is he." (vv. 11b–12)

Still in the dark about what's going on, David is approached by the aged Samuel, who pours oil over his auburn locks.[2] And from that day forward, David is never again the same.

> Then Samuel took the horn of oil and anointed him in the midst of his brothers; and the Spirit of the Lord came mightily upon David from that day forward. (v. 13a)

C. David's distinctive. David was not only anointed with oil, but with the Holy Spirit. And it was this that kept him humble. After his anointing, David didn't run out to try on crowns or

---

1. One of the most helpful resources on building self-respect into your children is *Hide or Seek,* by James Dobson (Old Tappan, N.J.: Fleming H. Revell Co., 1974).

2. Jewish historian Josephus tells us that while anointing David, Samuel whispered to him that he would be the next king.

shine up his chariot and ride through Bethlehem announcing his new position of royalty. He didn't even bronze a horn to hang in his tent. But David's humility shone like the sheen of his freshly anointed head...as he immediately went back to the fields with the sheep until God's scheduled inauguration.

> ### The Rewards of a Humble Heart
> The meek will he guide in judgment: and the meek will he teach his way.
>
> The meek shall inherit the earth; and shall delight themselves in the abundance of peace. (Ps. 25:9, 37:11—KJV)

IV. God Speaks, We Apply

From our study, we've seen that God looks beyond the outward appearance to the heart; He rejects the people-pleasers and exalts the God-pleasers. So take heart—God notices the nobodies. Let's wrap up this lesson with three applications.

A. God's solutions are often strange and simple . . . be open. Even though God's ways may not make sense to us, we need to be ready to be used by Him however He chooses.

B. God's provisions are usually sudden and surprising . . . be ready. At any moment, God may decide to promote you from a keeping-of-the-sheep role to a kingly one. Be ready and willing to be promoted for His kingdom.

C. God's selections are sovereign and sure. Nothing can be more stable than those decisions influenced by God.

> ### The Day David Was Noticed
> F. B. Meyer describes the day of David's anointing:
> It began like any ordinary day. No angel-trumpet heralded it; no faces looked out of heaven; the sun arose that morning according to his wont over the purple walls of the hills of Moab, making the cloud-curtains saffron and gold. With the first glimmer of light the boy was on his way to lead his flock to pasture-lands heavy with dew. As the morning hours sped onwards, many duties would engross his watchful soul—strengthening the weak, healing that which was sick, binding up that which was broken, and seeking that which was lost; or the

music of his song may have filled the listening air.[3]

It began like any other day—in 1020 B.C. or 1809 or our present year. Routine. Ordinary. Unassuming. Just the kind of day God chooses to use the lowly Davids to rule His kingdoms ... or the kind of day He will use to work unexpected graces in your life.

 Living Insights

Study One ▬▬▬▬▬▬▬▬▬▬▬▬▬▬▬▬▬▬▬▬▬

First Samuel 16:1–13 is a banner of hope to all nobodies. God's selection of David defied human reasoning, but perfectly fulfilled God's plan.

- Have you tried to put yourself in David's sandals that day? How about Samuel's? Or Jesse's? Choose one character from our passage and write down what that day might have been like from his perspective.

A Day in the Life of _____

_____

_____

_____

_____

_____

_____

_____

_____

_____

_____

_____

_____

_____

3. F. B. Meyer, *David* (Grand Rapids, Mich.: Zondervan Publishing House, 1953), pp. 15–16.

Living Insights

Though we've learned many practical lessons, we could easily fail to apply them. Use the following statements to zero in on your life. Be open and objective.

● In 1 Samuel 16:2, we see Samuel afraid of Saul. Do you have a Saul in your life—someone who intimidates you? Write down that person's name. How have you been handling this situation? Has it been pleasing to the Lord? Could you be dealing with it in a better way? Think about this, reflecting on what God's Word says about fear.

● What do you look for in people? Do you concentrate on externals or internals? Circle the characteristics that are important to you as you make choices involving people.

Education	Integrity
Financial Status	Physical Appearance
Character	Sensitivity
Walk with God	Intelligence
Attitudes	Popularity

● Jesse didn't have an equal appreciation for the members of his family. Do you? Jot down a few of the ways that you show them you value them equally. Jesse also failed to foster mutual respect among his family. Have you? Write down some ways that you can encourage a bond of respect in your home.

_____

_____

_____

_____

_____

_____

_____

Soft Music for a Hard Heart

1 Samuel 16:14–23

The words of eighteenth-century English dramatist William Congreve sound a truth that touches us all:

> Music has charms to soothe a savage breast,
> To soften rocks, or bend a knotted oak.[1]

From an infant whose hot, tear-streaked face is cooled by a mother's tender lullaby to a corporate ladder-climbing executive whose stiff deadlines are suppled by the sweet strains of Tchaikovsky—music works its healing power in all of us.

Its ability to soothe our terror, soften our hard spots, and bend our rigid, gnarled souls is nothing new. David, the young king-elect, besides being a faithful shepherd and man of valor, was a skilled musician. And one day, God called him from the tranquil pastures to the tumultuous palace to favor the disturbed King Saul with the therapy of his music.

I. Saul's Strange Malady

Saul's disorder was the direct result of two actions God took against him:

> Now the Spirit of the Lord departed from Saul, and an evil spirit from the Lord terrorized him. (1 Sam. 16:14)

A. Departure of the Lord's Spirit. The Lord's Spirit left Saul,[2] and the king came to know the terrible vacuum of His absence. Many believers read this passage and are afraid that the Holy Spirit might leave them as well. But this fear can be erased by recognizing Pentecost as the pivotal point in the Spirit's ministry. Before Pentecost, the Holy Spirit's presence was rarely permanent, usually coming only for special circumstances and needs. However, since Pentecost (Acts 2:1–4) the indwelling of the Holy Spirit in believers is permanent (see John 14:16, Eph. 4:30, Rom. 8:9b). Believers today will never be left to work out their salvation without the help of the Spirit.[3]

---

1. As quoted in *Bartlett's Familiar Quotations,* 14th ed., rev. and enl., ed. Emily Morison Beck (Boston, Mass.: Little, Brown and Co., 1968), pp. 391–92.

2. References to the Spirit departing from a believer are found only in the Old Testament. Some examples are David's fear that the Holy Spirit would be taken from him after his encounter with Bathsheba (Ps. 51:11) and Samson's predicament after he had yielded to Delilah's enticement: "[he] did not know that the Lord had departed from him" (Judg. 16:20).

3. For a helpful discussion on the permanence of the Holy Spirit's indwelling, see *The Holy Spirit,* by Charles Caldwell Ryrie (Chicago, Ill.: Moody Press, 1965), pp. 68–69.

B. Terror of an evil spirit. That Saul was being terrorized by an evil spirit was no secret to anyone within earshot of his chambers. His own servants diagnosed the problem for him:

> "Behold now, an evil spirit from God is terrorizing you." (1 Sam. 16:15)

The word *terrorize* comes from the Hebrew word *baath,* meaning "to fall upon, startle, overwhelm."[4] Saul was utterly overwhelmed by this spirit sent by the Lord. Many find it puzzling that God would send an evil spirit to a believer. But, as Merrill Unger explains:

> The Spirit departed from Saul, and an evil spirit, that is, a demon, began to torment the rejected king by the Lord's permission. Divine sovereignty controls evil forces for God's purposes. Believers who stubbornly reject God's Word and go on in self-will and rebellion expose themselves to demon control to a greater or lesser degree.... Saul is patently a case of demonization (commonly called demon possession).[5]

Our Demonic Age

Satan thrives in our present era, his dark deeds often excused as "temporary insanities." Wife and child abuse, shooting rampages, serial killings—those who commit such crimes often explain that they were overwhelmed or overcome by some compelling force or emotion and simply lost control. And Satan is the silent, unnamed victor.

The only power strong enough to combat Satan and his hosts is the Holy Spirit. As John tells all believers:

> You are from God, little children, and have overcome them; because greater is He who is in you than he who is in the world. (1 John 4:4)

When we give Christ the controls of our lives, He will triumph over the darkest forces of evil!

II. David's Unique Ability

Tormented by an evil spirit, Saul's "savage breast" needed soothing. When Saul's servants identified his malady, they prescribed music as the cure.

---

4. Job used this same root word to describe the day of his birth (Job 3:5). And David used it twice when he spoke of being overwhelmed by "torrents of destruction" (2 Sam. 22:5).

5. Merrill F. Unger, *Unger's Commentary on the Old Testament* (Chicago, Ill.: Moody Press, 1981), vol. 1, p. 385.

"Let our lord now command your servants who are before you. Let them seek a man who is a skillful player on the harp; and it shall come about when the evil spirit from God is on you, that he shall play the harp with his hand, and you will be well." (1 Sam. 16:16)

A. Description of David's qualifications and skills. Desperate, Saul agreed to the suggested prescription without hesitation.

So Saul said to his servants, "Provide for me now a man who can play well, and bring him to me." (v. 17)

And David's name was the first to come to his servants' minds.

Then one of the young men answered and said, "Behold, I have seen a son of Jesse the Bethlehemite who is a skillful musician, a mighty man of valor, a warrior, one prudent in speech, and a handsome man; and the Lord is with him." (v. 18)

Not a bad résumé. It's interesting that with David's list of impressive qualifications, it was his skill on the lyre[6] that brought him to the king's chamber, where Saul would grow to respect and love him. God used David's musical skill to bring him one step closer to the throne.

Are You Available?

Never discount any aptitude, talent, or gift that God has given you, even those that have grown dusty on the shelves of the past. God can brush them off and use them in incredible ways. The only thing He asks is that we be available—like David, who set down the lamb in his arms and picked up his harp because he was asked to.

How available are you? When God asks you to use your talents, do you argue or do you, without hesitation, say yes?

B. Invitation to the palace. Impressed by David's credentials, Saul sent for the young shepherd.

So Saul sent messengers to Jesse, and said, "Send me your son David who is with the flock." And Jesse took a donkey loaded with bread and a jug of wine and a

---

6. The lyre, or harp, was a stringed instrument used primarily for worship (see Ps. 33:2, 57:7–9, 81:2, 92:1–3, 108:1–2). It most likely consisted of strings stretched across an open frame, perpendicular to the sound board. See *The Eerdman's Bible Dictionary,* ed. Allen C. Myers (Grand Rapids, Mich.: William B. Eerdmans Publishing Co., 1987), p. 463.

young goat, and sent them to Saul by David his son. (vv. 19–20)

David didn't know it, but he was on his way to see Saul so he could learn how to be king.

C. Position with the king. Here comes David on a loaded-down donkey—king-elect with no inkling of protocol, no court savvy, no understanding of political pressures or class distinctions. But it didn't take long for David to make a place for himself in Saul's court—and in his heart.

> Then David came to Saul and attended him, and Saul loved him greatly; and he became his armor bearer. And Saul sent to Jesse, saying, "Let David now stand before me; for he has found favor in my sight." (vv. 21–22)

Although he was to be Saul's successor, David didn't compete with Saul or try to elbow him off the throne. Once a faithful shepherd, he was now a faithful servant, humble and supportive, willing to use his gifts.

Proverbs 18:16
> A man's gift makes room for him,
> And brings him before great men.

III. Music's Effective Ministry

Whenever Saul writhed in his madness, David would pick up his harp and play till Saul's spirit was quieted.

> So it came about whenever the evil spirit from God came to Saul, David would take the harp and play it with his hand; and Saul would be refreshed and be well, and the evil spirit would depart from him. (1 Sam. 16:23)

Why did Saul love David? Because his music brought refreshment and relief to his life.

Stretcher-Bearers

If you minister to people in their misery and malady, then, like David in the eyes of Saul, you will be beloved in their sight. An unbreakable clasp fastens your lives together as you extend a hand of restoration to their lives.

Are you willing to minister to the needy ... to bear the stretcher for a crushed spirit, to salve a heart's open wounds (see Gal. 6:2, Rom. 15:1, Matt. 25:32–40)?[7]

---

7. If you'd like to learn more about becoming a "stretcher-bearer," a fine source is Michael Slater's book *Stretcher Bearers* (Ventura, Calif.: Regal Books, 1985).

IV. Our Immediate Responsibility

Just as certain kinds of music can unleash our caged feelings, other types can entrap our spirits and actually hinder our growth in Christ. It's our responsibility to screen the musical messages we receive. For the world's music blares through its quadriphonic speaker system the message of carnality—a message that may harden even a heart once tender toward the Lord.

 Living Insights

We have seen some of the power of music in this tender story of Saul and David. But other Scriptures talk about music too. Let's look at a few. As the biblical orchestra assembles before you, conduct a search for God's theme in each reference. This may be a prelude to a whole new song in your life!

References	Themes
2 Chron. 5:11–14	
Ps. 40:3	
Ps. 119:54	
Ps. 150	
1 Cor. 14:8–9	
Col. 3:16	

Living Insights

Some tough questions are being raised about music today, so Christians need to be clear in their thinking. Use your notes from the previous study to help you think through the following issues. Try these as discussion starters with family members or close friends.

- What kind of music do you like? Why do you like it? How does it make you feel when you're listening to it, and after?

- Think of someone who has a different musical preference than you. Does this particular style bother you? Why? Does the Bible say anything about this type of music? Do you think it is wrong for this person to enjoy that style? Why or why not?

- Ask God for wisdom in this area of your life.

David and the Dwarf
1 Samuel 17

In 1501, an unformed block of crudely-cut marble lay untouched in a cathedral workshop in Italy.

By the beginning of 1504, Michelangelo had transformed it into the *David,* which today, at Florence's Galleria dell' Accademia, towers as his largest sculpture.

In this 13½-foot statue, the sculptor has embodied

> all the passionate drama of man's inner nature. The sinews of the neck seem to tense and relax, the veins of the neck, hands, and wrists to fill, the nostrils to pinch, the belly muscles to contract and the chest to lift with the intake of breath, the nipples to shrink and erect, the whole proud being to quiver like a war horse that smells the battle. But of the nature of the battle there is no indication whatever; it is eternal and in every man.[1]

Indeed, in the *David,* Michelangelo has made stone to breathe, and not only as a symbol of humanity's inner nature but specifically of Israel's David.

Chiseled into the giant statue's stony body are some of the qualities that marked David as a man of God. The knitted brow, eyes at once liquid and fiery, powerful hands—these display David's solid-marble strength, his colossal character, his larger-than-life faith. Even the slingshot slung over his shoulder symbolizes not *action* but *attribute*—in battle the young warrior relied not upon his meager material resources but upon the abundant power of the Lord.

In this lesson, we will turn to the chapter in David's life where he meets Goliath in the valley of Elah.

And we'll find out who the *real* giant was.

I. Goliath: Front and Center
A. The battleground (1 Sam. 17:1–3).
Picture the scene. A vast canyon enclosed by mountains on both sides. The Philistines on one side, the Israelites on the other, like blankets of humanity thrown across the mountains' shoulders. But the battle wasn't to be between two armies, but between two representatives—one from each side of the valley.

---

1. Frederick Hartt, *Michelangelo: The Complete Sculpture* (New York, N.Y.: Harry N. Abrams, Inc., Publishers, n.d.), p. 114.

B. The champion. Goliath, the Philistine hero, was no small man. In verse 4, we read:

> Then a champion came out from the armies of the Philistines named Goliath, from Gath, whose height was six cubits and a span.

Not only was he huge, he appeared impenetrable—all 9½ feet of him was armored and weaponed to the hilt.

> And he had a bronze helmet on his head, and he was clothed with scale-armor which weighed five thousand shekels of bronze.[2] He also had bronze greaves on his legs and a bronze javelin slung between his shoulders. And the shaft of his spear was like a weaver's beam, and the head of his spear weighed six hundred shekels of iron;[3] his shield-carrier also walked before him. (vv. 5–7)

Even his words were mercilessly intimidating.

> And he stood and shouted to the ranks of Israel, and said to them, "Why do you come out to draw up in battle array? Am I not the Philistine and you servants of Saul? Choose a man for yourselves and let him come down to me. If he is able to fight with me and kill me, then we will become your servants; but if I prevail against him and kill him, then you shall become our servants and serve us." Again the Philistine said, "I defy the ranks of Israel this day; give me a man that we may fight together." (vv. 8–10)

The giant gave his challenge, not just once, but twice a day for forty days (v. 16).

Personal Giants

The Goliaths in our lives attack us daily, relentlessly. Whether people, pressures, worries, or fears, they consistently yell across our personal valleys of Elah a challenge that rattles the foundations of our hearts. But God will be faithful to deliver us. And if we will put our trust in Him, we will be able to echo David's song:

> "I love Thee, O Lord, my strength."
> The Lord is my rock and my fortress and my deliverer,
> My God, my rock, in whom I take refuge;

---

2. Approximately 200 pounds.

3. Approximately 25 pounds.

> My shield and the horn of my salvation, my
>   stronghold.
> I call upon the Lord, who is worthy to be praised,
> And I am saved from my enemies. (Ps. 18:1–3)

II. Enter: David, "The Giant"

The scene suddenly shifts from the threatening battleground to the quiet hamlet of Bethlehem.

A. At home. While David's three oldest brothers were off serving Saul in battle, David traveled back and forth between soothing Saul and tending sheep, apparently unaware of Goliath's challenge (1 Sam. 17:12–15).

B. With the soldiers. Jesse, knowing the impending danger in the valley, became concerned about his sons and sent David to check on them and take them some food (vv. 17–19). Notice that David was not sent to fight, but to be a messenger. When he got to the battleground, however, he found himself smack-dab in the middle of the war. His mission took him to the front lines of battle, where Goliath, making his daily appearance, could be clearly heard (vv. 22–23). When the Israelites saw Goliath, they huddled together like frightened sheep. But rather than frightening David, the giant's challenge roused his respect for the Lord.

> Then David spoke to the men who were standing by
>   him, saying, "What will be done for the man who kills
>   this Philistine, and takes away the reproach from
>   Israel?[4] For who is this uncircumcised Philistine, that
>   he should taunt the armies of the living God?" (v. 26)

Overhearing David's conversation with the soldiers, his brother Eliab—with acidic envy and a razor-blade tongue—attacks David's motives.

> "Why have you come down? And with whom have you
>   left those few sheep in the wilderness? I know your
>   insolence and the wickedness of your heart; for you
>   have come down in order to see the battle." (v. 28b)

Notice the slam. But David, displaying his giant faith, refused to be offended. He simply turned away from his brother and back to more important things—his desire to protect God's people and the integrity of His name.

---

4. Saul, who had neglected his responsibility to fight Goliath, offered a reward for anyone who would accept the challenge. This reward included financial gain, the king's daughter, and freedom from taxation for his father's household (v. 25b).

┌─ *Learning to Walk* ─────────────────────────────────────┐

Most people on the battlefield that day saw only one man—Goliath.

But David saw the Lord.

God was as real to David as Goliath was to the soldiers. But, where the soldiers walked by sight, petrified by Goliath's size, David walked by faith and was moved to obedience by the awesomeness of God's character.

What about you? Are you a soldier . . . or a David? Do you walk clumsily, holding to the flimsy handrail of sight and appearances? Or have you learned to stand firmly on the rock-solid foundation of faith (see Heb. 11:6)?

C. **Before Saul.** Full of confidence—the fruit of faith—David volunteered to fight Goliath.

> And David said to Saul, "Let no man's heart fail on account of him; your servant will go and fight with this Philistine." (v. 32)

But David's offer wasn't accepted without an argument.

> Then Saul said to David, "You are not able to go against this Philistine to fight with him; for you are but a youth while he has been a warrior from his youth." (v. 33)

Saul is hung up on the externals. But David is sure of his inner source of strength. He convinces Saul with stories of the miraculous ways God delivered him in the past.

> "Your servant was tending his father's sheep. When a lion or a bear came and took a lamb from the flock, I went out after him and attacked him, and rescued it from his mouth; and when he rose up against me, I seized him by his beard and struck him and killed him. Your servant has killed both the lion and the bear; and this uncircumcised Philistine will be like one of them, since he has taunted the armies of the living God." And David said, "The Lord who delivered me from the paw of the lion and from the paw of the bear, He will deliver me from the hand of this Philistine." (vv. 34–37a)

┌─ *Never Forget the Lion and the Bear* ────────────────────┐

In a sermon on this passage, C. H. Spurgeon made a poignant observation.

> These were noteworthy facts which David had stored up in his memory, and he now mentions

> them, for they exactly answered his purpose.
> We ought not to be unmindful of the way by
> which the Lord our God has led us, for if we
> are we shall lose much. Some saints have very
> short memories. It has been well said that we
> write our benefits in dust and our injuries in
> marble, and it is equally true that we generally
> inscribe our afflictions upon brass, while the
> records of the deliverances of God are written
> in water. It ought not so to be. If our memories
> were more tenacious of the merciful visitations
> of our God, our faith would often be strength-
> ened in times of trial. Now, what did David rec-
> ollect, for I want you to remember the same.[5]

How could Saul argue against so sure a faith? He couldn't.

> And Saul said to David, "Go, and may the Lord be
> with you." (v. 37b)

But before letting David go to the battleground, Saul thought he
needed to equip him with some armor.

> Then Saul clothed David with his garments and put
> a bronze helmet on his head, and he clothed him
> with armor. (v. 38)

It must have been a sight—David, a 36 regular, wearing the
armor of Saul, a 52 long. It didn't stay on David very long.

> And David girded his sword over his armor and tried
> to walk, for he had not tested them. So David said to
> Saul, "I cannot go with these, for I have not tested
> them." And David took them off. (v. 39)

David's trust was neither in the shield nor the sword, but in the
living God.

III. Exit: Goliath, "The Dwarf"

David's battle with Goliath was brief and brilliant.

A. Warming up. Armed only with five stones gathered from the
ravine's brook, David approached Goliath. And after Goliath
mocked his lean defense (vv. 43–44), David made his fatal
weapon known.

> Then David said to the Philistine, "You come to me
> with a sword, a spear, and a javelin, but I come to
> you in the name of the Lord of hosts, the God of the
> armies of Israel, whom you have taunted." (v. 45)

---

5. Charles Haddon Spurgeon, *The Treasury of the Bible* (Grand Rapids, Mich.: Zondervan
Publishing House, 1968), vol. 1, p. 660.

B. Looking up. Then, with all boldness and faith, David made known his strategy and purpose.

> "This day the Lord will deliver you up into my hands, and I will strike you down and remove your head from you. And I will give the dead bodies of the army of the Philistines this day to the birds of the sky and the wild beasts of the earth, *that all the earth may know that there is a God in Israel,* and that all this assembly may know that the Lord does not deliver by sword or by spear; *for the battle is the Lord's* and He will give you into our hands." (vv. 46–47, emphasis added)

David lived by the philosophy that "the battle is the Lord's." Is that your philosophy? Or do you try to fight your own battles, outsmart the enemy on your own? God honors those who let Him fight their battles (Heb. 10:30). Only *He* will triumph over all our enemies!

C. Wrapping up. W. Phillip Keller describes the brief battle scene of 1 Samuel 17:48–51 with color and passion.

> With a rush, like a leopard leaping to the attack, David launched himself up the hill toward Goliath. The sling whistled ominously as he whirled it over his head. Then the thong was released. The stone struck!
>
> The next instant the giant crashed down the slope, face forward. The blood spurted from the skull shattered by the rock. It was as if he had been struck by a bullet.
>
> David rushed up to the prostrate form as Goliath's armorbearer fled in panic. Picking up the giant's massive sword he severed his head, the blood and gore spurting from the jugular vein.
>
> In triumph David stood upon the huge hulk. The battle was over! The daring deed was done! It was an instant of intense elation for all Israel....
>
> What all of Saul's military might had been unable to achieve, a single shepherd had done with simple faith in God.[6]

D. Mopping up. With their "unconquerable" hero conquered, the Philistines fled. The Israelites chased and killed them, covering the valley's floor with the bodies of the slain (v. 52). David

---

6. W. Phillip Keller, *David: The Time of Saul's Tyranny* (Waco, Tex.: Word Books, 1985), vol. 1, pp. 92–93.

brought Goliath's head back to Jerusalem and hung the giant's weapons in his tent as trophies of the battle the Lord had won (v. 54).

IV. Finale: Reminders for Today's Battles

Goliath lives on as a symbol of the giants each of us faces in our own lives. The following are reminders to not only help us see our Goliaths, but with God's help, to slay them as well.

A. **Facing giants is an intimidating experience.** David saw through eyes of faith, but Goliath still looked gigantic. Faith doesn't blind us to the externals, but enables us to see beyond them as we draw on God's power.

B. **Doing battle is a lonely experience.** Your Goliaths are *your* Goliaths. In fact, they may not be gigantic to anyone else but you; and no pastor, counselor, or friend can tell you what should or should not be a giant in your life. You and the Lord have got to fight them alone.

C. **Trusting God is a stabilizing experience.** In battle against Goliath, David didn't let the jitters interfere. When you turn a giant over to God, it's amazing how stable you can be.

D. **Winning victories is a memorable experience.** In David's battle, the truth came out. Goliath was the dwarf, and David the true giant.

The Giant with the Soft Heart

While Michelangelo's *David* was still just a block of marble, it earned the name "the giant." The sculpture may be surrealistic in size, but it's a true-to-life symbol of the giant character, devotion, and faith God chiseled into David's soul.

In Michelangelo's prayer to the Sculptor, surely the heart of David can be heard:

Lord, in the extreme hours,
Extend to me Thy pitying arms,
Take me from myself and make of me one to
please Thee.[7]

---

7. As quoted by Hartt in *Michelangelo: The Complete Sculpture,* p. 300.

Living Insights

We all have our Goliaths. They are with us morning and evening, day after day, taking over our territory. Saul tried to equip David with his own armor, but it didn't fit. However, God has provided a suit of armor tailor-made for His children!

● Ephesians 6:10–17 explains the armor in detail. Use this passage of Scripture to determine what is represented by each piece of armor. Then go one step further and jot down how you can apply each item. You may find particular areas in your life that need more protection.

The Armor of God—Ephesians 6:10–17

"Girded your loins"   Attribute: _____

_____

_____

Application: _____

_____

_____

"Breastplate"   Attribute: _____

_____

_____

Application: _____

_____

_____

"Shod your feet"   Attribute: _____

_____

_____

Application: _____

_____

_____

Continued on next page

"Shield"   Attribute: _____

_____

_____

Application: _____

_____

_____

"Helmet"   Attribute: _____

_____

_____

Application: _____

_____

_____

"Sword"   Attribute: _____

_____

_____

Application: _____

_____

_____

 Living Insights

Study Two ▬▬▬▬▬▬▬▬▬▬▬▬▬▬▬▬▬▬▬▬▬▬▬▬▬▬▬▬

It's not enough to know our defense. We also need to know our enemy.

- In Study One we looked at our armor. Now let's look at our adversary. What is the giant in your life? Do you have a plan for defeating it? Does David's battle remind you of any in your past where you came out victorious? What part do you let God play in this warfare? Spend some time working through a battle plan for defeating the Goliath in your life.

Personal Battle Plan

Enemy: _____

Past victories to remember: _____

_____

_____

_____

_____

_____

God's rank in this battle (General? Corporal? Private?): _____

_____

Strategy for attack: _____

_____

_____

_____

_____

_____

_____

_____

_____

_____

_____

_____

_____

_____

_____

_____

Aftermath of a Giant-Killing
1 Samuel 17:55–18:9

Often, the toughest trials come just after the victory. Incredible amounts of opposition, pressure, and even pain can follow in the wake of all the trophies and ribbons and roses.

This was David's experience.

Following Goliath's death, in the backwash of that miraculous victory, he stepped into another arena that put his faith and character to the test.

In this lesson we will examine the aftermath of David's battle—the effects he experienced before his trophies had even begun to gather dust.

I. Review: A Giant Slain
In our childhood memories of Bible stories, David's killing of Goliath stands out as the high-water mark of his life. And it seems that this victory inaugurated his reign as Israel's king and that his life stayed on an even keel from then on. But Scripture tells a different story. While the giant-killing was David's greatest achievement up to that time, it swept him out to a sea not of blissful kingship but of tumultuous testing—and he was adrift on that sea for many years. Before taking a look at this stormy period of David's life, let's review his victory and some of the positive things it brought him.

A. Remarkable achievement. David—not yet twenty years old and untrained in war—stepped out on the battlefield and faced Goliath, which neither Saul nor any of his men had dared to do. And with one fling of the slingshot, Goliath was dead.

B. Royal interest. In a flashback scene, where David was about to kill the giant, Saul asks his commander for some background on the courageous young man.

> Now when Saul saw David going out against the Philistine, he said to Abner the commander of the army, "Abner, whose son is this young man?" And Abner said, "By your life, O king, I do not know." And the king said, "You inquire whose son the youth is." (17:55–56)

Abner took immediate action to fulfill the king's request, and when David returned with Goliath's head in his hand, he took him straight to Saul.

> And Saul said to him, "Whose son are you, young man?" And David answered, "I am the son of your servant Jesse the Bethlehemite." (v. 58)

32

> **A Clarifying Note**
>
> Many Bible critics turn backflips at this passage, using it as proof that the Scriptures are contradictory and therefore unreliable. They argue that Saul had to have known who David was, since David was his personal musician, someone he had grown to love (16:21–22).
>
> The answer to this dilemma is that Saul's questions centered around the identity of David's father, not David himself. Saul needed to know David's father's name for two reasons. First, he probably wanted David as his personal bodyguard (18:2). Anybody who could whip a giant could certainly guard a king, but this would require his father's permission. And second, Saul wanted to keep his promise to the man who killed Goliath. He wanted to write the check, marry off his daughter, and free the man's father from taxation (17:25).[1]

C. Instant popularity. David's victory brought him esteem not only in the king's eyes but also in the eyes of the people. Overnight David was a national hero.

> So David went out wherever Saul sent him, and prospered; and Saul set him over the men of war. And it was pleasing in the sight of all the people and also in the sight of Saul's servants. (18:5; see also v. 16)

David was the king's favorite prodigy . . . until his popularity grew beyond Saul's. Soon the king's blood began to boil with fear and envy (v. 15).

II. Relationships: Four Different Experiences

In the aftermath of Goliath's death, God began to mold David into His man for the throne. He had to soften him, shape him, cast him, kiln him. And He used David's relationships as tools for the sculpting.

A. David before the people of Israel: exaltation. David's victory over Goliath won him a variety of receptive audiences.

1. **Saul.** David became the king's attendant and officer (v. 5a).
2. **Soldiers.** David became their commander (v. 5b).
3. **Servants.** Saul's servants watched David as he performed his duties in Saul's court (v. 5c).

---

1. Several other solutions to this difficult passage have been offered. Some critics note that an indefinite length of time had passed since David's last visit to the court and that perhaps David had lapsed out of Saul's memory. Others suggest that the mental state Saul was in when he last saw David was so disturbed that the king failed to recognize him. For a thorough discussion of this passage, see *Unger's Commentary on the Old Testament,* by Merrill F. Unger (Chicago, Ill.: Moody Press, 1981), vol. 1, p. 388.

4. Women. The women sang David's praises in the city streets.

> And the women sang as they played, and said,
> "Saul has slain his thousands,
> And David his ten thousands." (v. 7)

B. David under King Saul: submission. David submitted to Saul's authority graciously and sincerely. He made no mention that he was to be the new king ... poked no disloyal jabs ... took no presumptuous liberties ... made no attempt to out-king Saul. No, even after slinging that triumphant stone, David clung to his humility (see vv. 5, 30).

Humble Yourselves

Do you try to push your way up the ladder of notoriety? Or, like David, do you leave the lifting to God?

To be exalted requires only one thing of us ... that we humble ourselves before the Lord (see James 4:10, Luke 1:52).

C. David with Jonathan: affection. Aware of the rough waters David was about to face, God gave him an intimate friend in Saul's son Jonathan.

> The soul of Jonathan was knit to the soul of David,
> and Jonathan loved him as himself. (1 Sam. 18:1b)

Four qualities marked the deep friendship of these kindred spirits.

1. A willingness to sacrifice. At their first meeting, Jonathan gave his new friend a token of his devotion.

> Then Jonathan made a covenant with David because he loved him as himself. And Jonathan stripped himself of the robe that was on him and gave it to David, with his armor, including his sword and his bow and his belt. (vv. 3–4)

Merrill Unger gives us some background about Jonathan's gift of friendship.

> Clothing possessed something of the wearer's personality.... To receive any part of the dress that had been worn by a sovereign or his oldest son and heir was deemed the highest honor that could be conferred on a subject.... Jonathan, the king's son, gave all the material gifts. David, the poor man's son, gave only his love and respect.[2]

You can hardly impose on intimate friends. They are willing to give sacrificially—selflessness prevails in their hearts.

---

2. Unger, *Unger's Commentary on the Old Testament,* p. 388.

2. **A loyal defense.** When Saul eventually gave in to his murderous jealousy and sought to kill David, Jonathan defended his friend.

> Then Jonathan spoke well of David to Saul his father, and said to him, "Do not let the king sin against his servant David, since he has not sinned against you, and since his deeds have been very beneficial to you. For he took his life in his hand and struck the Philistine, and the Lord brought about a great deliverance for all Israel; you saw it and rejoiced. Why then will you sin against innocent blood, by putting David to death without a cause?" (19:4–5)

Jonathan's plea was not made as a son to his father, but as a man to his friend's enemy. A true friend is never two-faced, but will defend you out of loyalty and love.

3. **An accepting heart.** Because Saul persisted in trying to kill him, David needed to flee for his safety. Broken over having to leave his friend, David freely expressed the depth of his feelings to Jonathan.

> David rose from the south side and fell on his face to the ground, and bowed three times. And they kissed each other and wept together, but David more. (20:41b)

When your heart is bruised, an intimate friend will let you weep—freely and transparently.

4. **A consistent encouragement.** When David was on the run from Saul's malicious pursuit, Jonathan went to strengthen him.

> And Jonathan, Saul's son, arose and went to David at Horesh, and encouraged him in God. Thus he said to him, "Do not be afraid, because the hand of Saul my father shall not find you, and you will be king over Israel and I will be next to you; and Saul my father knows that also." (23:16–17)

No sermon. No scriptural rebuke. Just heart-to-heart, spirit-boosting encouragement.[3]

---

3. The charge that David and Jonathan's relationship was a homosexual one is completely erroneous. Their love for each other was little like the love between a man and a woman. It was above and beyond that. It was based on a kindred spirit in God, which enabled them to embrace and relate and love each other with His encouragement during life's low tides. It was beautiful, the most shameless of relationships.

Treasures

   Intimate friendships are like precious jewels, extremely valuable and hard to find.

   If polished consistently with the soft cloths of commitment, encouragement, and honesty, they will glisten and shine the invaluable worth of love.

D. Saul versus David: opposition. Hearing the women's song of praise to David, Saul's envy began to rage within him.

> Then Saul became very angry, for this saying displeased him; and he said, "They have ascribed to David ten thousands, but to me they have ascribed thousands. Now what more can he have but the kingdom?" And Saul looked at David with suspicion from that day on. (18:8–9)

Saul became jealous; his love and admiration for David turned into hatred and dread. David had done nothing to deserve Saul's mistreatment. He had only killed Goliath, which Saul himself had allowed. Yet God used this situation to further shape David's character, just as He uses unfair treatment in *our* lives.

God Never Promises That Life Will Be Fair

   Injustice is one of the hardest things to take in life. It's infuriating to see rogues run free while honest men suffer ... to watch the hard-hit get hit harder while the protected receive more protection.

   When you feel like life isn't treating you fairly, remember that God will let no trial go to waste. Take consolation in the fact that He is molding you into the image of Jesus. As James tells us:

> Consider it all joy, my brethren, when you encounter various trials, knowing that the testing of your faith produces endurance. And let endurance have its perfect result, that you may be perfect and complete, lacking in nothing. (James 1:2–4)

III. Relevance: Our Lives Today

Those of us in the dim aftermath of a bright victory can cling to three truths from this study.

A. Not knowing the future forces us to live one day at a time. David had no idea that the giant-killing would bring such intense opposition from Saul. He had to live one day at a time, taking things as they came and trusting God to prove Himself faithful.

B. Having a friend helps us face whatever comes our way. The encouragement of a close friend makes the valleys of our lives seem less vast, less threatening, less ominous.

C. A positive attitude and wisdom are the best defenses against an enemy. When you see your opposition coming, it's easy to start rolling up your mental sleeves, thinking about where to throw your first jab. But the best response to opposition is to stay even-tempered and let God fight your battles for you.

 Living Insights

Study One ▬▬▬▬▬▬▬▬▬▬▬▬▬▬▬▬▬▬▬▬▬▬▬▬▬▬▬▬▬▬

One of the most famous friendships in history is that of David and Jonathan. Their story is encouraging, isn't it? Since friendships are as important today as they were back then, let's do a little digging to see how we can improve our friendship skills.

- There are many admonitions in the New Testament regarding relationships. We really do need each other! Take a brief survey of these New Testament references and jot down your observations on friendship.

Responsibilities to Our Friends

John 13:34 _____

_____

Romans 12:10 _____

_____

Romans 14:13 _____

_____

Romans 15:7 _____

_____

1 Corinthians 12:25 _____

_____

Continued on next page

37

Galatians 6:2 _____

_____

Ephesians 5:21 _____

_____

Philippians 2:3 _____

_____

Colossians 3:16 _____

_____

1 Thessalonians 5:15 _____

_____

James 5:16 _____

_____

1 Peter 5:5 _____

_____

 Living Insights

Study Two ━━━━━━━━━━━━━━━━━━━━━━━━━━━━━━━

This lesson allowed us to study four common types of relationships. We've all experienced submission, affection, exaltation, and opposition. Let's give our relationships a second look.

- Are you currently occupying a role of submission? What makes it difficult? What are the advantages? Do you feel God is teaching you some valuable lessons through this relationship? If so, what are they?

- Do you have someone you'd call an intimate friend? What tells you this person is a true friend? What is the key to your friendship? What advice would you give to someone just beginning a friendship?

- Have you had an occasion to be exalted by others? How did you handle it? Think about some of the advantages and disadvantages.

- Opposition . . . are you experiencing it? David suffered for doing what was right. Has that happened to you? What kinds of thoughts go through your mind when things like this occur? What role does God play in these situations?

Every Crutch Removed

1 Samuel 18–21

Lying in the emergency room, hair still matted with clumps of ice, you hear the doctor explain that your leg has been broken in three places.

It was your first time ever to ride the ski lift—after snowplowing around on the bunny slope all morning—and you were euphoric! From your panoramic view, the sky looked swimming-pool blue and the snow blankets polar bear white; the witty wind whipped through your hair and nipped at your nose.

Your elation quickly turned to paranoia as you skied off the lift and faced what looked to you more like a cliff than a slope. But, knowing there was only one way down, you took a deep breath and began snaking your way cautiously through the powder.

Suddenly, you heard the whoosh of skis slicing the ice and a "Look Ouuuuut!" A goggled monster, bearing a SKI TEAM decal on his cap, was coming straight at you.

Next, shivering blackness.

And now, surrounded by the smell of freshly cast plaster, you face the prospect of months on crutches.

Crutches—those wooden legs with cushioned arm pads—will be your sole support. You will lean on them while your bones are healing, depend on them to support every feeble step you take.

Not everyone has broken a leg, yet we all have some broken places in our emotional bones. Weaknesses, vulnerabilities, cracks in our character that make us lean on crutches when blown down by life's icy blasts.

But, unlike wooden crutches, our emotional crutches won't speed up the healing process. In fact, they'll retard it. So, now and then, God moves in and takes away every support but Himself. The process is painful, but the result is a healing that pleases God. In this lesson, we catch David in the process.

I. Truth about Our Crutches
Before looking at David's crutches and how God removed them, we'll expose how our crutches hamper our spiritual healing and growth.

A. They become substitutes for the Lord. Isaiah 41:10 says:

> " 'Do not fear for I am with you;
> Do not anxiously look about you, for I am your God.
> I will strengthen you, surely I will help you,
> Surely I will uphold you with My righteous right
>   hand.' "

Why look to someone or something else to support you when God, righteous and powerful, is willing and ready to uphold you?

B. They keep our focus horizontal. Human crutches paralyze our walk of faith. When we look to those around us for support, we fix our eyes on a human plane. And our godly, vertical perspective is lost in the hazy horizon.

C. They offer only temporary relief. Like aspirin to a broken bone, human crutches relieve the discomfort and pain of a crisis only temporarily.

II. Removal of David's Crutches

The crisis David faced put a limp in his spirit, making him desperate for support. Never before had he been so vulnerable—and never again would he live free from the memory of brokenness and pain.

A. Crisis reviewed. Saul, David's superior, had turned against him. Because of his miraculous victory over the Philistine giant, David had won the Israelites' favor (1 Sam. 18:6–7, 16), which angered Saul and made him burn with envy (vv. 8–9, 14–15). Soon after, while David was playing his harp for the disturbed king, Saul hurled a spear at David, trying to pin him to the wall (vv. 10–11). At this, David fled. But Saul's vendetta against him continued. When he couldn't kill David himself, he put him into battles where he might be killed by the Philistines (v. 17). When that failed, Saul's next plan was to ensnare David by having him marry his daughter, Michal (vv. 20–21). But when that plan backfired (vv. 28–29), Saul put out a contract on his life.

B. Crutches removed. Because of the emotionally crippling crisis David was facing, he clung to several supports. And even though David had done nothing to warrant Saul's vengeful treatment, God still chose to pull the crutches away from him, one at a time.

    1. Crutch one: David's position. David had been promoted to a place of military leadership; he had led in battle as Saul's trusted officer. And now he was fleeing from Saul's sword (19:8–10), never to return to his position as the king's heroic soldier.

    2. Crutch two: David's wife. Saul pursued David right to his home, where he was with Michal, his wife. The night before David was to be killed, Michal helped him escape (vv. 11–12).

But her loyalty proved false. When asked by her father why she let David go, she explained that he had threatened to kill her if she didn't help him (v. 17). Looking out for her own interests, Michal betrayed David, never offering one word in his defense. Another crutch knocked out from under him.

3. **Crutch three: David's mentor.** David fled straight to Samuel, who had anointed him and to whom David looked for guidance. After he explained to Samuel the details of Saul's pursuit, Samuel suggested they both take refuge in Naioth. But Saul discovered their hiding place (v. 19). So again David fled (20:1a), leaving behind the security of his mentor, Samuel.

4. **Crutch four: David's friend.** From Naioth, David fled to Jonathan, his closest friend. In this scene, we can see that the bones of David's emotional security have begun to fissure. David asks his friend:

> "What have I done? What is my iniquity? And what
> is my sin before your father, that he is seeking
> my life?" (v. 1b)

Jonathan assures David that he will not die (v. 2), but at this point, David is not to be comforted. Saul's fiery eyes and the whir of the hurled spear are still fresh in his mind.

> Yet David vowed again, saying, "Your father knows
> well that I have found favor in your sight, and he
> has said, 'Do not let Jonathan know this, lest he
> be grieved.' But truly as the Lord lives and as
> your soul lives, there is hardly a step between
> me and death." (v. 3)

Because of the danger, Jonathan and David decided to part. Perhaps this was David's most painful loss—separation from his closest friend.

5. **Crutch five: David's self-respect.** After seeing Ahimelech, priest of Nob (21:1), David fled to Gath—Goliath's hometown (v. 10). And the people immediately recognized him as the giant's killer.

> But the servants of Achish said to him, "Is this
> not David the king of the land? Did they not sing
> of this one as they danced, saying,
> 'Saul has slain his thousands,
> And David his ten thousands'?" (v. 11)

David's desperation swelled as he was once again seized by fear. Take a look at the demeaning act he put on:

> So he disguised his sanity before them, and acted
> insanely in their hands, and scribbled on the

doors of the gate, and let his saliva run down
into his beard. (v. 13)

With this performance, David lost his final crutch—he could
no longer lean on the simple support of even his own self-
respect.

III. Lessons in Leaning for Cripples to Learn

**A. There is nothing wrong with leaning if you're leaning
on the Lord.** We've got to lean on something or somebody;
life brings too many heartbreaking experiences to go it alone.
We are built to be leaners—leaners not on our spouses, friends,
jobs, reputations, or ourselves, but on the Lord. Solomon reminds us:

Trust in the Lord with all your heart,
And do not lean on your own understanding.
(Prov. 3:5)

The crutches of human understanding are fragile and frail; they
cannot withstand the blizzards life brings to our hearts. But
God's support is strong and sure; He is our refuge from the
storm (Isa. 25:4).

**B. Being stripped of all crutches is one of the most
painful of life's experiences.** Like those with just-broken
legs who misplace their crutches, those whose human supports
have been removed feel incredible helplessness, loneliness, and
pain.

A Concluding Thought

People on crutches amble awkwardly and uncomfort-
ably. They endure itchy limbs, sore armpits, and long, hard,
frustrating days.

In the same way, we who are supported by human
crutches sacrifice greatly for our dependency. The race
toward a mature faith is reduced to a hobble; the prize of
wholeness, delayed (see Heb. 12:1, 1 Cor. 9:24).

When your spiritual bones have been broken, when the
ligaments of your soul have been twisted and torn—lean
on Jesus. He is the only one whose support will never fail
you, whose comfort will pick you up in life's crises and
help you stand (see Deut. 33:27a, 2 Cor. 1:3).

Living Insights

Study One ▬▬▬▬▬▬▬▬▬▬▬▬▬▬▬▬▬▬▬▬▬▬▬▬

We've surveyed three chapters of 1 Samuel, looking specifically at what David's crutches were. Now let's use this study to look at all of 1 Samuel 18–21.

● Take some time to read each chapter, jotting down questions that come to mind as well as significant words and phrases. Perhaps you'd like to develop another theme from these chapters—for example, the friendship of David and Jonathan. Don't be in a hurry. Allow God to speak to you. End this time of study by giving God thanks for your discoveries.

1 Samuel 18–21

_____

_____

_____

_____

_____

_____

_____

_____

_____

_____

_____

_____

_____

_____

_____

_____

_____

Continued on next page

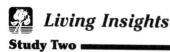 *Living Insights*

Crutches ... substitutes for God. A casual glance around should convince us that many Christians are leaning on the wrong supports. How about you? Let's venture into this sensitive area.

● Listed below are the crutches we discovered in our lesson. Using this list as a springboard, think of some crutches you've seen in others' lives or your own life. Add them to this list of substitutes for God.

☐ Position	☐ Self-respect
☐ Mate	☐ _____
☐ Mentor	☐ _____
☐ Friend	☐ _____

● Now put a check in the box by the ones that pose the greatest threat to your walk with God. Perhaps, now that you're more aware of your crutches, you can begin shifting your dependence to Him.

For Cave Dwellers Only
1 Samuel 22:1–2, Selected Psalms

Few historical events paint a picture as black and bitter as those that surrounded the Nazi regime, when Hitler persecuted, tortured, and mercilessly killed millions of Jews.

Yet, even during those years of abysmal darkness, the light of protection and security flickered through. On the top floor of their crooked little Dutch house, Corrie ten Boom and her family built a secret room to provide a hiding place for many of those hunted people.

Over a period of time, hundreds of Jews passed to safety through the walls of the ten Booms' home, until one chilling February day when the secret was whispered into the Gestapo's greedy ear. Within days, Corrie was torn from her comfortable home in Haarlem and locked in a dank prison cell in Scheveningen.

Once a provider of safety, Corrie herself now needed a hiding place. And although no secret room was to be found in the prisons and concentration camps at Scheveningen, Vught, or Ravensbruck, she sheltered her soul in the Lord.

David also suffered undeserved persecution, bringing him to one of the lowest, most desperate points of his life.

And like Corrie, David also found a hiding place . . . in the dark, damp cave of Adullam, David saw the light of God's deliverance.

I. The Cave

Fleeing from Saul's angry sword, David sought refuge in the cave of Adullam. With all the crutches in his life taken from him, he havened his body within the walls of the rocky cavern; and his spirit, within the clefts of God's granite love. While in the cave, David composed this song.

> I cry aloud with my voice to the Lord;
> I make supplication with my voice to the Lord.
> I pour out my complaint before Him;
> I declare my trouble before Him.
> When my spirit was overwhelmed within me,
> Thou didst know my path. . . .
> I cried out to Thee, O Lord;
> I said, "Thou art my refuge,
> My portion in the land of the living.
> Give heed to my cry,
> For I am brought very low;
> Deliver me from my persecutors,

For they are too strong for me.
Bring my soul out of prison,
So that I may give thanks to Thy name;
The righteous will surround me,
For Thou wilt deal bountifully with me."[1]
(Ps. 142:1–3a, 5–7)

> **A Caveman After God's Own Heart?**
>
> Being a person after God's heart doesn't mean never experiencing the concentration camp or the despair of the cave. It means being able to sing in the silent darkness like David did, confident that one day God will deal bountifully with you again.

II. The Challenge

God seldom leaves us to rest in our hiding places alone. Instead, He brings us the challenge of sharing our protection with others. To Corrie ten Boom, He brought officers, guards, and other suffering prisoners with whom she could share her hope in Jesus. To David, He brought four hundred desperate men who needed his leadership.

A. Being with others. David found his cave filled with family as well as strangers—all refugees from Saul's faulty leadership.

> So David departed from there and escaped to the cave of Adullam; and when his brothers and all his father's household heard of it, they went down there to him. And everyone who was in distress, and everyone who was in debt, and everyone who was discontented, gathered to him; and he became captain over them. Now there were about four hundred men with him. (1 Sam. 22:1–2)

B. Seeing the needs. The whole nation ached under Saul's heavy-handed rule. Of the four hundred who joined David in the cave, some were under great pressures and stresses, others were in debt due to Saul's heavy taxation, and still others were discontented—they'd been wronged and mistreated, and their spirits were beginning to sour. David didn't walk away from these men; instead, he accepted the challenge of meeting their needs, and the group increased from four hundred to six hundred men (23:13).

C. Accepting the leadership. Recognizing their needs, David gave of himself to meet them. He became the group's leader,

---

1. The superscription of this psalm reads "Maskil of David," meaning "a teaching of David." It was David's desire that we learn from the psalm that spilled from his heart in that dark cave.

instilling character and direction in their lives. He trained them to be mighty warriors, the very strength of Israel.

A Thought to Consider

During one of the darkest points of David's life, God gave him a ministry—helping six hundred men, who had been weakened by despair, to become strong warriors.

In our lives, too, God often uses cave experiences to give us purpose and direction. So next time you find yourself in the cave, be aware of how God may be wanting to use you. Prepare yourself to be brought out of that cavern and into a new ministry!

III. The Change

Before we wrap up this lesson, let's analyze David's radical change from lonely desperation to God-entrusted leadership. Three reasons explain why God showed David, in a cave of despair, the bright light of deliverance.

A. He admitted his need. David openly expressed to God his cavernous fear and loneliness (see Ps. 142).

B. He cried out for help. Psalm 57 shows us the depth of his pain—and of his faith.

> Be gracious to me, O God, be gracious to me,
> For my soul takes refuge in Thee;
> And in the shadow of Thy wings I will take refuge,
> Until destruction passes by.
> I will cry to God Most High,
> To God who accomplishes all things for me.
> He will send from heaven and save me;
> He reproaches him who tramples upon me.
> God will send forth His lovingkindness and His truth.
> My soul is among lions;
> I must lie among those who breathe forth fire,
> Even the sons of men, whose teeth are spears and
> arrows,
> And their tongue a sharp sword.
> Be exalted above the heavens, O God;
> Let Thy glory be above all the earth.
> (vv. 1–5)

C. He had a teachable spirit. Throughout David's life, he had learned that in all situations God was his protector and deliverer. He had tasted of God's deliverance again and again. And the memory of that taste lingered forever in his heart. Shortly before fleeing to the cave of Adullam, when he feigned insanity before Achish and God mercifully delivered him, David showed his teachable spirit when he composed this psalm.

O taste and see that the Lord is good;
How blessed is the man who takes refuge in Him!
O fear the Lord, you His saints;
For to those who fear Him, there is no want.
The young lions do lack and suffer hunger;
But they who seek the Lord shall not be in want of
     any good thing....
Many are the afflictions of the righteous;
But the Lord delivers him out of them all....
The Lord redeems the soul of His servants;
And none of those who take refuge in Him will be
     condemned.
(Ps. 34:8–10, 19, 22)

Songs of Deliverance

Like David, whose songs reverberated a message of faith and hope within the cave's rocky walls, Corrie ten Boom, too, sang songs that attested to God's deliverance.

Because she took refuge in the secret room of God's love, her spirit was never quelled. Even when confined in a cold, gray, solitary cell in Scheveningen, she sang songs that were bright and rich with joy.

Most likely, you will never have to seek refuge from the cruelty of a concentration camp or the sword of an angry king. But as God's child, there are enemies all around whom you will need to flee from—temptations, weaknesses, people who would trample your faith.

When faced with an enemy, remember that God has a secret place for you—a place of protection, comfort, and direction for your life. There He will put a song of deliverance in your heart.

You are my hiding place
You shelter me from the snares of my enemies
And surround me with
     sweet songs of deliverance that
     balm the bitter wounds
          of my despair
I will trust in You, yes
I will trust in You
For there in Your safe and secret place

> You will sing over my broken spirit
> And You will make me whole[2]
>
> —Julie Martin

 Living Insights

Study One ▬▬▬▬▬▬▬▬▬▬▬▬▬▬▬▬▬▬▬▬▬▬▬▬▬▬

Did you ever wonder how David felt while in the cave? Scripture gives us a peek into his diary.

- Psalms 57 and 142 reveal David's feelings. Let's take this opportunity to draw personal insights from these portions of the Word. Can you relate to David's feelings? How does he respond to God? To his situation? Jot down your observations.

Observations	
Psalm 57	Psalm 142

 Living Insights

Study Two ▬▬▬▬▬▬▬▬▬▬▬▬▬▬▬▬▬▬▬▬▬▬▬▬▬▬

Both David and Corrie ten Boom were sensitive to God during the dark times of their lives. Because they looked to Him, God was able to bring them into the light of their own unique ministry. Are you tender enough toward God to let Him lead you through your pain and use you in a new way in the lives of others? Turn your eyes to God in your despair and you will find His hope shining bright and sure, piercing through your darkest times.

---

2. Based on Psalms 31:12 and 32:7.

Life's Most Subtle Temptation
1 Samuel 24

Revenge surreptitiously wraps its thistly branches around all of us. And when it does, even the most forgiving, most peaceful of people will become beasts.

In his masterpiece *Othello,* Shakespeare vividly portrays the universal temptation to retaliate.

Iago, ensign in the Venetian army, hates his general, Othello. When Othello promotes young and handsome Cassio over him, Iago plants a labyrinthine thicket of lies to ensnare Othello in the thorns of revenge.

Iago begins his plot by planting a seed of distrust in Othello's mind concerning his bride's faithfulness, framing Cassio as her lover. This tiny seed of jealousy sprouts into a tangled, tragic nightmare. Iago's plan is consummated when he murders a man and wounds Cassio—and when Othello suffocates his innocent Desdemona . . . and takes his own life.

Lies, murder, suicide—all because of Iago's frustrated ambition, his hunger for power, and his slighted pride.

Like Iago, David must have felt that his superior, Saul, had wronged him: out of jealousy and anger, Saul had reduced David's position from right-hand man to refugee.

In this lesson, we catch David with the opportunity to give Saul a bitter taste of revenge. But we'll see that David's response to this tugging temptation is ultimately a sweet sacrifice of love to the Lord.

I. Hard Facts to Face about Revenge
Before delving into David's life, let's look at our own urge to get even with the Sauls in our lives.
A. What we call it. We frequently soften hard-core revenge in our minds by labeling it with a couple of "more acceptable" terms.
1. **"My rights."** This label represents the thinking, I have my rights. I'm no doormat. I refuse to lie down and be walked on.
2. **"Justified retaliation."** Much like the first label, this one says, I've been wronged and I've got to stick up for what's right. Justice must prevail!
B. How God feels about it. Whatever we call it, God calls it revenge. And His feelings toward it are anything but ambivalent.
> Never pay back evil for evil to anyone. Respect what is right in the sight of all men. If possible, so far as it depends on you, be at peace with all men. Never

take your own revenge, beloved, but leave room for
the wrath of God, for it is written, "Vengeance is Mine,
I will repay," says the Lord. (Rom. 12:17–19; see also
Deut. 32:35–36)

If there's to be any vengeance, God commands us to leave it in
His hands.

C. Why we do it. We seek revenge because we have suffered an
injury, like the slighted Iago when Othello gave his promotion
to Cassio. Then we look for a vulnerability in our offender. Iago
knew Othello's soft spot was jealousy; so, acting out his depravity, he attacked Othello's trust in Desdemona. The pattern
of revenge always begins with an injury and is completed when
our offender has been bruised in return.[1]

II. A Biblical Case Study: David and Saul

We have already seen that Saul had injured David. Now, in 1 Samuel 24,
David finds Saul in a vulnerable position and is tantalized by the
temptation to avenge himself.

A. The situation. When we last looked at David's life, we found
him in the cave of Adullam, surrounded by a band of hundreds
of men who were faithful to him as their captain (22:1–2). Since
then, David and his men had saved the town of Keilah from the
Philistines, fled from Saul and his army, and been saved by the
bell when a Philistine raid took Saul's attention off of David
(chap. 23). Now we find David and his men safely camouflaged
in the cool caves of Engedi, temporarily out of Saul's reach. But
tenacious Saul gets wind of David's whereabouts.

Now it came about when Saul returned from pursuing
the Philistines, he was told, saying, "Behold, David is
in the wilderness of Engedi." Then Saul took three
thousand chosen men from all Israel, and went to
seek David and his men in front of the Rocks of the
Wild Goats. (24:1–2)

Three thousand men? Chosen from all Israel? It's clear that Saul
means business.

B. The temptation. While in pursuit of David, Saul stepped into
a cave to "relieve himself" (v. 3a). Little did he know that David
and his men were hiding in the darkness of that same cave (v. 3b).
For the first time since he had injured David, Saul was vulnerable.

1. Man's encouragement. Once David's men saw that Saul
was vulnerable, their human natures went into overdrive.

1. This pattern can be traced back to the first recorded case of revenge. God rejected Cain's
sacrifice and accepted Abel's (injury to Cain). Cain found Abel alone in the field (vulnerability
of Abel). And Cain killed Abel (depravity of Cain).

Their words, masked by a veil of spirituality, encouraged David to retaliate.

> And the men of David said to him, "Behold, this is the day of which the Lord said to you, 'Behold; I am about to give your enemy into your hand, and you shall do to him as it seems good to you.'" (v. 4a)

Something to Think About

Often, God gets blamed for things He has nothing to do with.

David's soldiers excused their desire to get even with Saul by saying it was God's timing, His will.

What about you? Are you harboring a sin in your life—a behavior with your spouse or children, a small selfishness, a bit of carnal character—rationalizing it as somehow being "God's way" or "part of His plan for you"?

---

2. **Human nature's response.** David couldn't completely give up this opportunity to get even. He had to come close enough to get at least a taste of the sweetness of revenge.

> Then David arose and cut off the edge of Saul's robe secretly. (v. 4b)

3. **The conscience at work.** David had barely slid his knife back into its sheath when God pricked his conscience (v. 5).

> So he said to his men, "Far be it from me because of the Lord that I should do this thing to my lord, the Lord's anointed, to stretch out my hand against him, since he is the Lord's anointed." (v. 6)

David was sensitive to even the little sins—sins we often don't take seriously. In fact, he felt so strongly about his small act of revenge that he confessed it before his men and persuaded them to leave the vengeance to God.

> And David persuaded[2] his men with these words and did not allow them to rise up against Saul. And Saul arose, left the cave, and went on his way. (v. 7)

---

2. The Hebrew word for *persuaded* means "torn apart." Because of David's conviction, his men, too, were torn up about their desire to get even with Saul.

> ### Contagious Conviction
>
> Like David, are you bold enough to stand up for your convictions—even when those in your office, family, or neighborhood strongly oppose them? Why not challenge them to godly living by your example? Nothing preachy. Nothing pushy. Just clean, sincere living.
>
> God honors those who stand up for His principles. And who knows, because of your godly lifestyle, others just might be persuaded to stand with you.

C. The conversation. Because David refused to get even with Saul, God blessed him. As a sidelight, look at the promise God gives us in Proverbs 16:7:

> When a man's ways are pleasing to the Lord,
> He makes even his enemies to be at peace with him.

Let's see how God brings peace between David and Saul through their conversation in the cliffs.

   1. David to Saul. When Saul left the cave, David followed him out to talk to him, torn garment in hand. He wanted to prove both his innocence and his integrity. The conversation begins with David openly displaying his respect for Saul.

> Now afterward David arose and went out of the cave and called after Saul, saying, "My lord the king!" And when Saul looked behind him, David bowed with his face to the ground and prostrated himself. (1 Sam. 24:8)

Next, David tries to set the record straight.

> And David said to Saul, "Why do you listen to the words of men, saying, 'Behold, David seeks to harm you'?" (v. 9)

Then, to his plea for innocence, he adds verbal and physical proof.

> "Behold, this day your eyes have seen that the Lord had given you today into my hand in the cave, and some said to kill you, but my eye had pity on you; and I said, 'I will not stretch out my hand against my lord, for he is the Lord's anointed.' Now, my father, see! Indeed, see the edge of your robe in my hand! For in that I cut off the edge of your robe and did not kill you, know and perceive that there is no evil or rebellion in my hands, and I have not sinned against you, though

you are lying in wait for my life to take it."
(vv. 10–11)

Finally, David told Saul he would let God judge between them (v. 12). More than revenge, David wanted the Lord's will to be done.

Confronting a Wrong

From a lesson like this, it would be easy to conclude that when we're injured or misunderstood, we're to sit back and swallow it. But the truth is, we do have a responsibility to confront, to stand up and declare the truth—not to get even, but to clear our consciences. The hard part comes afterward, when it becomes our responsibility to sit down and let God work in the other person's heart to make it right.[3]

---

2. **Saul to David.** David's honest words of confrontation tendered the tough-hearted Saul.

> Now it came about when David had finished speaking these words to Saul, that Saul said, "Is this your voice, my son David?" Then Saul lifted up his voice and wept. And he said to David, "You are more righteous than I; for you have dealt well with me, while I have dealt wickedly with you. And you have declared today that you have done good to me, that the Lord delivered me into your hand and yet you did not kill me. For if a man finds his enemy, will he let him go away safely? May the Lord therefore reward you with good in return for what you have done to me this day. And now, behold, I know that you shall surely be king, and that the kingdom of Israel shall be established in your hand." (vv. 16–20)

At the end of his reply, Saul makes a plea, and the two men depart in peace.

> "So now swear to me by the Lord that you will not cut off my descendants after me, and that you will not destroy my name from my father's household." And David swore to Saul. And Saul went to his home, but David and his men went up to the stronghold. (vv. 21–22)

---

3. For an excellent discussion on the value of confrontation, see *Caring Enough to Confront*, rev. ed., by David Augsburger (Ventura, Calif.: Regal Books, 1981).

III. Tough Principles to Practice

Revenge is as old as human nature. And, while not all vengeance creates a tragedy as bitter as Shakespeare's *Othello,* it all makes a travesty of God's control in our lives. If you're forming a plot of revenge, however small and insignificant you may think it to be, surrender it now. Release your grip on your get-even plan, and place the control in God's hands. Let's reflect on some principles that will help us relinquish our desire for revenge.

A. Since man is depraved, expect to be mistreated. The same human nature that beat in Saul's heart beats in all our hearts. We are only responsible for making sure we're not mistreating others.

B. Since mistreatment by others is inevitable, we can anticipate our feelings of revenge. If we're aware that the urge to get even will come, our guard will be up when we're wronged, and we'll be less likely to impulsively lash back.

C. Since the temptation toward revenge is predictable, refuse to fight in the flesh. While feelings of revenge are sometimes automatic, we don't have to act on them. With God's strength, we can surrender the desire to retaliate even before it begins.

 Living Insights

Study One ▬▬▬▬▬▬▬▬▬▬▬▬▬▬▬▬▬▬▬▬▬▬▬▬

Revenge . . . Scripture speaks directly to this subject. Listed below are some references that address this matter head-on. Next to each reference write your observations about the topic of revenge.

Revenge—Life's Most Subtle Temptation

Deuteronomy 32:35 _____

_____

_____

Psalm 94 _____

_____

_____

Continued on next page

Proverbs 20:22 _____

_____

_____

Proverbs 25:21–22 _____

_____

_____

Romans 12:17–21 _____

_____

_____

Romans 14:19 _____

_____

_____

Living Insights

Study Two

Would you agree that revenge is life's most subtle temptation? Let's look at this subject in a little more detail and try to personalize its impact in our lives.

- In your own words, define *revenge*. Compare your definition with that of a dictionary. How does revenge manifest itself in your life? What are the telltale signs that show you you're feeling revengeful? Do you feel better prepared to face this temptation after this lesson? Why or why not?

_____

_____

_____

_____

_____

_____

- Are you holding resentment against someone? Are you ready to reconcile? Why not make this your prayer today:

> Dear God,
>
> I acknowledge this moment that Jesus Christ took my sins when He didn't deserve them. I confess to You that I am resentful of _____. Even though Jesus died for me and my sins, I am holding against _____ the treatment he/she has given to me. Please forgive me. And help me to forgive _____. I ask You to free me from this bondage and help me to claim Your power through Jesus Christ my Lord.
>
> In His name,
>
> _____
> *Your Signature*

What to Feed an Angry Man

1 Samuel 25

The rays of each sunrise bring new opportunities to be taken and new choices to be made.

Yet, while each day carries with it a certain aura of adventure and growth and the possibility of success, it also brings the painful possibility of failure. Though God's mercies are new every morning, so are Satan's schemes.

Yesterday's victories may become today's temptations; the sin we shunned yesterday, we may embrace today.

Sunday's unconditional love can turn to Monday's selfishness.

A tender, forgiving heart can become punitive and tough.

And a refusal to retaliate can turn to cold-blooded revenge.

Like the rest of us, David learned the hard way that you can't live today on yesterday's obedience. In our last lesson, he chose to leave vengeance in God's hands; in today's scene, he is overcome by hotheaded impetuosity and nearly commits murder.

However, this story doesn't end in the shedding of blood, but in an outpouring of grace. Let's take a look at David in one of his most human moments—and at the woman God used to turn his hostile heart back to Himself.

I. Background Information

The conflict that incensed David was a fractured employer-employee relationship. David's boss failed to maintain an agreement, but instead of just going on strike, David plots to kill him.

A. David and his men. Under David's leadership, the hundreds of men from the cave of Adullam had been turned into a tight-knit band of guerrilla-like fighters, roaming the wilderness of Paran to protect shepherds from the predatory raids of the desert's wild tribes.

B. Sheep and the situation. It was a common custom—much like our present-day practice of tipping waitresses—that when the sheep were sheared, the owner of the flock would pay a portion of his profit to those who had protected his shepherds. David and his men had been working for Nabal, a wealthy man who had three thousand sheep and a thousand goats (1 Sam. 25:2). But when it was sheepshearing time, he wouldn't pay up.

II. Main Characters

This story develops like a one-act play, unfolding in several scenes. But before revealing its Broadway plot, let's make ourselves familiar with the main characters.

A. Nabal (vv. 3b, 17b, 25). A list of Nabal's qualities reveals that he was probably not the most popular man on the block. He was stubborn and harsh and dishonest in his dealings. In Hebrew, his name means "fool"; Nabal lived his life as if there were no God.

B. Abigail (v. 3a). If ever a marriage proved the adage that opposites attract, Nabal and Abigail's did. Unlike her husband, Abigail was intelligent—clear-thinking and wise. She was also physically attractive; a rare blend of inner and outer beauty.[1]

C. David (vv. 14–16). David and his men had faithfully protected Nabal's shepherds in the fields. But because Nabal refused to repay him, a fiery conflict developed.

III. Natural Conflicts

Along with the conflict between David and Nabal, two others help thicken this plot: one between Nabal and Abigail; the other between David's conscience and his temper.

A. Between husband and wife. As we've seen, Nabal and Abigail aren't exactly two peas in a pod. They differ vastly in temperament, attitude, and philosophy of life. Most likely, serious conflict infected their marriage.

B. Between employer and employee. This problem develops at sheepshearing time, when David sends his men to Nabal to collect their share of the profit.

> So David sent ten young men, and David said to the young men, "Go up to Carmel, visit Nabal and greet him in my name; and thus you shall say, 'Have a long life, peace be to you, and peace be to your house, and peace be to all that you have. And now I have heard that you have shearers; now your shepherds have been with us and we have not insulted them, nor have they missed anything all the days they were in Carmel. Ask your young men and they will tell you. Therefore let my young men find favor in your eyes, for we have come on a festive day. Please give whatever you find at hand to your servants and to your son David.' " (vv. 5–8)

---

1. The name Abigail means " 'whose father is joy,' no doubt giving a clue to her sunny, joyous, and gracious personality. Just the opposite of her husband, she was generous, kind, and lovely." From *Unger's Commentary on the Old Testament,* by Merrill F. Unger (Chicago, Ill.: Moody Press, 1981), vol. 1, p. 400.

But stingy Nabal refuses their gracious request, leaving David both hungry and insulted.

> But Nabal answered David's servants, and said, "Who is David? And who is the son of Jesse? There are many servants today who are each breaking away from his master. Shall I then take my bread and my water and my meat that I have slaughtered for my shearers, and give it to men whose origin I do not know?" (vv. 10–11)

Nabal's belligerent response boils David's blood.

C. Between David's conscience and his anger. David had controlled his anger toward Saul, refusing to take revenge against him. But for some reason, this mistreatment is too much for passionate David. Past victories are eclipsed by his vengeful plot to murder Nabal.

IV. Conflict Development

With nothing short of murder on his mind, David heads himself for a personal tragedy.

A. David's order is given.

> And David said to his men, "Each of you gird on his sword." So each man girded on his sword. And David also girded on his sword, and about four hundred men went up behind David while two hundred stayed with the baggage. (v. 13)

What happened to the cool, calm, and collected David who refused to murder Saul?

Temptation—New Every Day

"David! David! What is wrong with you? Why, one of the most wonderful things we have learned about you recently is your patience with Saul. You learned to wait upon the Lord, you refused to lift your hand to touch the Lord's anointed, although he had been your enemy for so many years. But now, look at you! Your self-restraint has gone to pieces and a few insulting words from a fool of a man like Nabal has made you see red! David, what's the matter?"[2]

The problem with David is the same problem we all face. Every day temptation assaults us, especially in areas where we have recently gained a victory. So every day we must offer a new prayer to God, asking that He deliver us afresh from sin's snare.

---

2. Alan Redpath, *The Making of a Man of God: Studies in the Life of David* (Westwood, N.J.: Fleming H. Revell Co., 1962), p. 107.

B. Abigail is informed. While David and his men are on their way to kill Nabal, one of Nabal's shepherds lets Abigail in on the plot.

> But one of the young men told Abigail, Nabal's wife, saying, "Behold, David sent messengers from the wilderness to greet our master, and he scorned them. Yet the men were very good to us, and we were not insulted, nor did we miss anything as long as we went about with them, while we were in the fields. They were a wall to us both by night and by day, all the time we were with them tending the sheep. Now therefore, know and consider what you should do, for evil is plotted against our master and against all his household; and he is such a worthless man that no one can speak to him." (vv. 14–17)

C. Abigail responds wisely. Even though her husband is "worthless," Abigail protects him. This loyal wife comes up with an ingenious plan that will both sate David's hunger and abate his anger.

> Then Abigail hurried and took two hundred loaves of bread and two jugs of wine and five sheep already prepared and five measures of roasted grain and a hundred clusters of raisins and two hundred cakes of figs, and loaded them on donkeys. And she said to her young men, "Go on before me; behold, I am coming after you." But she did not tell her husband Nabal. (vv. 18–19)

Talk about a Proverbs 31 woman! Within moments after hearing about David's plot to kill Nabal, Abigail organizes a full-scale catering service. Dinner via donkey for six hundred men.

D. David expresses anger. Meanwhile, David has not yet reached Nabal. But his vengeful words reveal that his fingers still itch to put the sword to Nabal's throat.

> Now David had said, "Surely in vain I have guarded all that this man has in the wilderness, so that nothing was missed of all that belonged to him; and he has returned me evil for good. May God do so to the enemies of David, and more also, if by morning I leave as much as one male of any who belong to him." (vv. 21–22)

E. Abigail appeals graciously. David's temper sizzles—until he is met by Nabal's wife.

> When Abigail saw David, she hurried and dismounted from her donkey, and fell on her face before David, and bowed herself to the ground. (v. 23)

Abigail was wise in her approach. Knowing David was angry, she had planned a speech that would crack the tough shell of his hostility.

> And she fell at his feet and said, "On me alone, my lord, be the blame. And please let your maidservant speak to you, and listen to the words of your maidservant. Please do not let my lord pay attention to this worthless man, Nabal, for as his name is, so is he. Nabal is his name and folly is with him; but I your maidservant did not see the young men of my lord whom you sent." (vv. 24–25)

In Abigail's plea we also see her faith. She credits God for keeping David from sin, pointing him back to the Lord.

> "Now therefore, my lord, as the Lord lives, and as your soul lives, since the Lord has restrained you from shedding blood, and from avenging yourself by your own hand, now then let your enemies, and those who seek evil against my lord, be as Nabal. And now let this gift which your maidservant has brought to my lord be given to the young men who accompany my lord. Please forgive the transgression of your maidservant; for the Lord will certainly make for my lord an enduring house, because my lord is fighting the battles of the Lord, and evil shall not be found in you all your days." (vv. 26–28)

Perhaps she makes her most poignant point when she reminds David that he's next in line for the throne and that, consequently, he needs to keep his record clear.

> "And it shall come about when the Lord shall do for my lord according to all the good that He has spoken concerning you, and shall appoint you ruler over Israel, that this will not cause grief or a troubled heart to my lord, both by having shed blood without cause and by my lord having avenged himself. When the Lord shall deal well with my lord, then remember your maidservant." (vv. 30–31)

F. David responds humbly. David's raging heart is stilled by Abigail's plea, his eyes once again fixed on the Lord.

> Then David said to Abigail, "Blessed be the Lord God of Israel, who sent you this day to meet me, and blessed be your discernment, and blessed be you, who have kept me this day from bloodshed, and from avenging myself by my own hand." (vv. 32–33)

After David assured Abigail that he had granted her request, she went home to find Nabal drunk, so she didn't tell him what had happened until morning (vv. 35–36). When she did, "his heart died within him so that he became as a stone" (v. 37). And it wasn't but ten days later that God struck him dead (v. 38).

Still a Man After God's Own Heart

Even though David sinned in his anger toward Nabal, he remained teachable and willing to change . . . a man after God's own heart.

It's not perfection that melds our hearts to God's—it's humility. And that quality of heart will lead us to admit our sin and to cry out with a cracked and broken voice, Blessed be the Lord who has lavished me with forgiveness and grace.

V. A Practical Principle for Seeing Supernatural Solutions

We all have days when we run across Nabals—those people Satan uses to nudge us into sin. But during those times of testing, God will send an Abigail—a messenger of His grace—to turn our sin-specked eyes back to Himself. Yesterday's victories don't have to become today's defeats. There's a principle that can help you keep your fresh, new days from becoming spiritual disasters: *When conflicts arise, be wise.* A wise response to conflict means looking at both sides of the problem, restraining yourself from being hasty, and praying.

"Watch and Pray . . ."

In a sermon on this slice of David's life, Charles Spurgeon makes the following comments:

Learn from this, dear brethren, that the best of men need to be always on the watch, lest, in some sudden temptation, they should be carried off their feet. You may fancy that you have no occasion to fear certain forms of temptation, but you do not know what you may do. The wall of resolution may be strong in one particular wind; but let the wind only blow from another quarter, and the wall may speedily fall. You may think yourself to be strong simply because, as yet, you have not been tested and tried as you will be sooner or later; and then, in a single moment, when you are least prepared for it, you may be overthrown. Remember our Lord's words to His disciples, "What I say unto you I say

---

unto all, Watch"; for, in such an hour as ye think not, temptation may come upon you; and woe be unto you if you are not found watching. Therefore, commit yourselves unto the Lord, and "watch and pray, that ye enter not into temptation."[3]

 Living Insights

Study One ▬▬▬▬▬▬▬▬▬▬▬▬▬▬▬▬▬▬▬▬▬▬▬▬▬

An angry man, a rare woman, and a fool...almost sounds like a pilot for a new TV show, doesn't it? Yet this cast of characters can teach us valuable lessons.

• Let's focus our attention on these three people and their character traits. Read through 1 Samuel 25 and, as you do, write down the personality characteristics of David, Abigail, and Nabal. Jot down the references too. End by drawing some conclusions about the character of each of these three people. What insights do they teach us today?

David		
Verses	Characteristics	Conclusions

---

3. Charles Haddon Spurgeon, *The Treasury of the Bible* (Grand Rapids, Mich.: Zondervan Publishing House, 1968), vol. 1, p. 676.

Abigail		
Verses	Characteristics	Conclusions

Nabal		
Verses	Characteristics	Conclusions

Continued on next page

![icon] Living Insights

In his book *Three Steps Forward, Two Steps Back,* Chuck Swindoll writes an entire chapter on anger, calling it the "burning fuse of hostility." Vivid picture, isn't it?

• Within that chapter, Chuck covers four ways to win over anger. Let's talk about them briefly.[4]

1. *Ignore petty disagreements.* Read Proverbs 17:14 and 19:11. According to these verses, how does anger begin? What should a Christian be doing when situations like these come up?

2. *Don't form close relationships with anger-prone people.* Read Proverbs 22:24–25. With whom do you spend time? Do you find yourself picking up their characteristics? What causes this to happen?

3. *Keep a close check on your speech.* Read Proverbs 15:1. What's the relationship between anger and your tongue? How would you describe your tongue in these recent days? Can you think of some ways you could improve on how you speak to others?

4. *Be honest in your communication . . . don't let anger build up.* Read Proverbs 27:4–6. What's difficult about the message of these verses? How would you describe your communication? How would your best friend describe it?

---

4. For a deeper look at the subject of anger, see *Three Steps Forward, Two Steps Back,* by Charles R. Swindoll (Nashville, Tenn.: Thomas Nelson Publishers, 1980), chap. 11.

Cloudy Days . . . Dark Nights

1 Samuel 27

The Pilgrim's Progress is a 300-year-old classic. An allegory of the Christian life, it was written from a prison cell. Penned by an uneducated tinker, its pages are now read in 101 languages.

The author is John Bunyan. Imprisoned twelve years for preaching the gospel without a license, he teaches us how to handle cloudy days and dark nights through a pilgrim named Christian.

Journeying from the City of Destruction to the Celestial City, Christian falls into a bog—a deep, miry, muddy hole called the Slough of Despond. His disloyal companion, Pliable, finds his way out and flees for home, leaving Christian to struggle alone. He cries out for rescue, and his groping hands meet the strong arms of Help—the Holy Spirit—who pulls him from the slough, sets him on his feet, and wipes the mud and slime of despondency from his brow.

David spent some time in that muddy hole too. There was nothing wrong with how he got into the bog; his problem started when he looked for his own way out.

I. Clouds and Darkness Come (1 Samuel 27:1–7)

There is nothing ethically, morally, or spiritually wrong with those feelings of despair that chill us like an unexpected downpour. It's when we run for cover in an enemy camp that disobedience begins. And that's where we find David in 1 Samuel 27.

A. The causes. David's dash toward disobedience had its feet on the starting block of distorted thinking.

1. **Humanistic viewpoint.** David was coming down from a roller coaster high. Twice he had the chance to kill his enemy Saul, and twice he passed it by. He'd had a chance to kill Nabal, but he listened instead to Abigail's advice. He was feeling righteous and victorious, and he was vulnerable to self's seductive voice. The first words of the chapter raise a warning flag: "Then David said to himself . . ." (v. 1a). When we listen to ourselves, it's important that we're saying the right things. David wasn't. He didn't look past the clouds in his sky; not once in this chapter does he seek God's perspective.

2. **Pessimistic reasoning.** David had his paintbrush out, and he was painting his horizon black. God had spoken through Samuel and said, "You're gonna be king." He had spoken through Abigail and the loyalty of Jonathan: "You're next for the throne." Even his enemy Saul had said, "I know I'm

looking at my replacement." But David—pious hero on the outside, doubting pouter on the inside—was convinced of the worst. Listen to his Eeyore drone:

"Now I will perish one day by the hand of Saul." (v. 1b)

3. **Rationalistic logic.** David's made-up problem led to a drastic solution.

"There is nothing better for me than to escape into the land of the Philistines. Saul then will despair of searching for me anymore in all the territory of Israel, and I will escape from his hand." (v. 1c)

The obvious hideout is the enemy camp in Philistine territory—the home of Goliath, where Saul wouldn't dare go. David's foot sprang off the starting block; he was off and running headlong toward disaster (vv. 2–3).

Who's Coming with You?

When our backs are against the wall . . . when we're tired of being good . . . when temptation presents tantalizing opportunities . . . it's easy to steel our hearts against a pricking conscience. Arrogant rationalization argues with weakening resolve: "So what if it's wrong. I'll pay the price. It won't hurt anyone but me."

That's what David thought. But when he fled to Philistia, he took six hundred men with him. Maybe he didn't invite them—but he had trained them. These men had joined forces with him at the cave of Adullam. They had done battle for him in the wilderness and among the border tribes. They looked up to him, took their cues from him. And they followed him into Philistia.

Not one of us lives only to ourselves . . . nor dies to ourselves . . . nor sins to ourselves.

Who is coming with you?

B. **The consequences.** David's panicky pessimism caused some serious repercussions.

1. **A false sense of security was created** (v. 4). Disobedience ought to bring remorse, but more often, at least initially, it brings exhilaration. That's how David felt. His plan worked. Saul called off the search. And David let out one huge sigh of relief.

Now it was told Saul that David had fled to Gath,
so he no longer searched for him.

Sin has its pleasures . . . but they are passing (Heb. 11:25b).
David felt safe in Philistia, but destruction was just around
the corner.

2. **The adversary's cause was adopted** (1 Sam. 27:5). David
meant to adopt a new home, not a new philosophy. But the
longer he splashed around in the bog, the less he wanted
to get out. Soon David, anointed king of Israel, was submit-
ting to an enemy king.

3. **A period of compromise was begun** (vv. 6–7). David
didn't just pitch a temporary tent in Philistia; he became a
resident. And during his sixteen-month stay, this sweet-
voiced singer of Israel was silent—his hymnbook contains
no psalms from this period of his life.

II. Winds and Storms Increase (1 Samuel 27:8–12)

David couldn't see the storm his sin was brewing, but the clouds
got darker and darker. The winds blew faster and the rains fell
harder, and pretty soon David was knee-deep in muddy mistakes.

A. Duplicity (vv. 8–9). David was an Israelite at heart, but he had
to act the part of a Philistine. He made military raids on neutral
tribes, giving the impression of championing Philistine causes
while doing Israel no harm.

B. Vagueness (v. 10). The facade was difficult to maintain. Soon
David was skirting the truth and finally out-and-out lying to
imply that he was raiding Israel.

C. Secrecy (vv. 11–12). Desperate to cover his tracks, David shred-
ded the evidence of his red-herring raids, killing every member
of the tribes he attacked. Double standards, half-truths, and
cover-ups became his way of life.

III. Injury and Devastation Occur (1 Samuel 29:1–30:6)

David found quick relief in his escape to Philistia. But instead of
leading him out of the muck, it took him four steps further into
despair.

A. He became displaced (29:1–7). King Achish was fooled by
David's deceit, but the commanders of the Philistine army began
to have their doubts. He was dismissed from his post as body-
guard of Achish. Now he was neither Israelite nor Philistine, a
man without an identity.

B. He became disillusioned (vv. 8–9). David had put his stock
in Achish's protection, and the deal fell through. He thought he
had the perfect setup, but his plan backfired. And he had no
Plan B to guarantee his safety.

C. He became distrusted (30:1–6). David had not only been granted asylum in Philistia, he had been given a measure of authority in a little stretch of land called Ziklag. But as he and his men trudged home, stripped of their purple hearts and ribbons of valor, they found their territory ash-gray and smoking, their families captured by Amalekites. The men turned on David, bitter and vengeful. He'd lost the remains of their respect.

D. He became distressed (v. 6a). With his men threatening to stone him, David sank into depression. His security was gone. The sides of the slough closed in around him.

IV. Timeless Truth

Entrenched in his slough of despond—displaced, disillusioned, distrusted, and distressed—David finally pulled back the clouds. After sixteen months of sinking his toes in soft, squishy sand, trying to make his home in the rain forest of despair, he finally reached out for Help's hand.

> But David strengthened himself in the Lord his God. (v. 6b)

John Bunyan's slough of despond was a prison cell; he turned it into a pulpit of hope. David's was an exhausting run for his life; he turned it into a chorus of compromise. But David finally learned what John Bunyan knew . . . that cloudy days and dark nights call for right thinking and vertical focus. The slough of despond is a quagmire on the path of every journeying Christian. Our tired feet slither and slip; our friends scatter like dry leaves; but Help—our Helper, the Holy Spirit—is never far.

 Living Insights

Study One ━━━━━━━━━━━━━━━━━━━━━━━━━━━━━━━━━

Those of us who are parents know that our children are our mirrors. We see in them not only our strengths but our weaknesses. Solomon went through a period of disillusionment much like his father David did in the passage we've been studying.

● The chart on the following page lists the characteristics of David's despondency from our lesson. Ecclesiastes is the record of his son Solomon's despair. Read Ecclesiastes 1–4, and see if you can find the ten symptoms of distress that we've seen in his dad. Jot down the verses for future reference.

David's Cloudy Days	Solomon's Dark Nights
1 Samuel 27	Ecclesiastes 1–4
Humanistic viewpoint (v. 1)	2:15
Pessimistic reasoning (v. 1)	
Rationalistic logic (v. 1)	
Hurting others (vv. 2–3)	
False sense of security (v. 4)	
Adopting the adversary's cause (v. 5)	
Lengthy period of compromise (vv. 6–7)	
Divided allegiance (vv. 8–9)	
Vagueness (v. 10)	
Secrecy (vv. 11–12)	

 Living Insights

Study Two ▬▬▬▬▬▬▬▬▬▬▬▬▬▬▬▬▬▬▬▬

Have you been making your home in the "Slough of Despond" lately? We've just seen from David's life that it's easy to fall into. Let's run some personal tests. In the privacy of your own heart, answer the following questions honestly and objectively. Check to see if you are on David's downward staircase.

- Are you feeling torn between two groups, or do you feel like you don't really belong in any group? How have feelings of displacement surfaced in your life?

- Have you recently experienced disillusionment? What were the circumstances? Were you looking to the right sources for satisfaction?

- Are you trusted by those who know you well? What are the reasons for their respect or lack of respect for you?

- Are you currently experiencing depression? Can you put your finger on its cause? Do you struggle with feelings of insecurity? How do you cope?

- How can right thinking and vertical focus work for you this week?

Two Deaths:
Analysis and Analogies
1 Samuel 31

Death marks an ending, but it also ushers in a beginning . . . the seeds of new life are scattered with the ashes of each death.

For example, the death of a parent breeds new responsibilities for a child. A spouse's death, a new lifestyle for the mate left behind. And the death of an infant can beget growth and the hope that soon another life will bud within the womb.

In our last few lessons, David has been in transition between his old life in the sheep fields and his new life on the throne. No longer shepherd but not yet king, David waits for God to deliver him into the royal world.

In today's study, we'll take a parenthetical look at the event that gave birth to David's reign—the death of King Saul. We will also draw some analogies between Saul's death and that of Jesus, which brings us a life that never ends.

I. Saul's Demise: Pathetic Tragedy

Few men have had beginnings as bright as Saul's. Physically, emotionally, spiritually, professionally—he had it all. Yet from that high and noble beginning, Saul sank to an infamous ending. His epitaph could have read,

"Behold, I have played the fool." (1 Sam. 26:21b)

Mirroring Saul's foolish, ungodly life is the tragic, pathetic way in which he died.

A. The battle: a slaughter.
Scripture never disguises the black truth in rose-colored cloaks. In 1 Samuel 31, we read about an ugly battle between Israel and Philistia—the battle that would be Saul's last.

> Now the Philistines were fighting against Israel, and the men of Israel fled from before the Philistines and fell slain on Mount Gilboa. And the Philistines overtook Saul and his sons; and the Philistines killed Jonathan and Abinadab and Malchi-shua the sons of Saul. And the battle went heavily against Saul, and the archers hit him; and he was badly wounded by the archers. Then Saul said to his armor bearer, "Draw your sword and pierce me through with it, lest these uncircumcised come and pierce me through and make sport of me." (vv. 1–4a)

Saul's fear of being humiliated outweighed his dread of dying. No sword could wound him as deeply as a slice to the heart of his pride.

B. The death: a suicide. Since his armor-bearer refused to kill him, Saul saw only one way out.

> So Saul took his sword and fell on it. (v. 4b)[1]

Preserving an Image

Even when facing death, Saul's main concern was to preserve his image in the enemy's eyes. He offered no prayer of repentance, no plea for help. His eyes were fixed on a horizontal plane of carnality . . . and on that plane, he died.

If you were to die today, which image would you try to preserve—an image of someone tough and impregnable in the eyes of the world . . . or of one repentant and forgiven in the eyes of God?

II. The Philistine's Response: Sadistic Brutality

Seeing that Saul was dead, the few Israelite survivors fled, and the Philistines moved in behind them to occupy Israeli cities (v. 7). In the activities that followed, the Philistines bannered their depravity high on the city walls.

A. Exploitation. Sifting through the bodies strewn across the land like litter along the highway, the Philistines found the corpses of Saul and his sons.

> And it came about on the next day when the Philistines came to strip the slain, that they found Saul and his three sons fallen on Mount Gilboa. And they cut off his head, and stripped off his weapons, and sent them throughout the land of the Philistines, to carry the good news to the house of their idols and to the people. And they put his weapons in the temple of Ashtaroth, and they fastened his body to the wall of Beth-shan. (vv. 8–10)

---

1. There is a chilling similarity between Saul's death and Adolf Hitler's. One of Hitler's greatest fears was being found dead by the enemy. He didn't want to be embalmed and then strutted around the allied countries to prove how futile his dictatorship was. So, when the time came for him to die, he and his wife sat in a room and carried out his plan. She swallowed a small capsule of poison, and Hitler shot himself in the mouth with a revolver. As part of his plan, Hitler had called his aides before the suicides so they would come and find them, take their bodies, douse them with gasoline, and burn them—so that no trace of their bodies would ever be found.

On that dark Philistine night, the four bodies hung still on the walls of Beth-shan.

> ### Tragedy and Irony
> The city of Beth-shan wasn't far from where the trumpet's blast had inaugurated Saul as king. During his forty-year reign, Saul gained no ground for his kingdom. Tragically, his lifetime of accomplishments were of little value.
>
> Symbolically speaking, when you die, will you be far from where you began your life in God's kingdom? Will there be miles of growth to mark the path of your spiritual journey?
>
> Will the kingdom have benefited because of your life?

B. Cremation. When the people of Jabesh-gilead heard how brutally the Philistines had treated the bodies of Saul and his sons, they showed a somber mercy.

> Now when the inhabitants of Jabesh-gilead heard what the Philistines had done to Saul, all the valiant men rose and walked all night, and took the body of Saul and the bodies of his sons from the wall of Beth-shan, and they came to Jabesh, and burned them there. And they took their bones and buried them under the tamarisk tree at Jabesh, and fasted seven days. (vv. 11–13)[2]

III. Saul's Death: Classic Analogy

Saul's death was the final step in David's ascent to the throne. But perhaps more importantly, it serves as an analogy to Christ's crucifixion. We hope that what you discover in the following chart will get you thinking about the new start Christ's death has brought you (Isa. 43:18–19a, 2 Cor. 5:17).

Saul's Death	Christ's Death
1. It appeared to be the end of all *national* hope.	1. It appeared to be the end of all *spiritual* hope.
2. It seemed as though the *adversary* had won the final victory.	2. It seemed as though *Satan* had won the final victory.

2. Since the Bible is silent on the issue of cremation, individual preferences in taking care of loved ones' remains should be respected, as long as God's peace reigns in the decision.

3. It paved the way for an entirely new plan of *operation*.	3. It paved the way for an entirely new plan of *salvation*.
4. It opened the throne room to *David*.	4. It opened the throne room to *sinners*.
5. It ended an era of *dissatisfaction* and *failure*.	5. It ended an era of *law* and *guilt*.
6. It displayed the *foolishness* of *man*.	6. It displayed the *"foolishness"* of *God* (1 Cor. 1:25).[3]

 Living Insights

Study One ▬▬▬▬▬▬▬▬▬▬▬▬▬▬▬▬▬▬▬▬▬▬▬

As we've seen in this lesson, death often brings the opportunity for new life. Saul's death ushered in David's reign, and Christ's death has given us the hope of eternal life.

- Let's take this time to study some of the *new* things we can experience because of Jesus' death. Look up the verses below, and write your observations in the space provided. Then thank God for this newness you can enjoy because He died for you.

John 3:16 (Salvation) _____

_____

_____

Acts 13:39 (Justification) _____

_____

_____

Romans 6:22 (Deliverance from Sin) _____

_____

_____

Continued on next page

---

3. For more information on this intriguing topic, see the study guide *Strong Reproofs for a Scandalous Church,* coauthored by Julie Martin, from the Bible-teaching ministry of Charles R. Swindoll (Fullerton, Calif.: Insight for Living, 1988), pp. 25–32.

1 Corinthians 15:54–57 (Victory over Death) _____

_____

_____

Isaiah 53:5 (Spiritual Healing) _____

_____

_____

 Living Insights

Study Two ━━━━━━━━━━━━━━━━━━━━━━━━━━━━━

Death—nothing causes us to think more seriously about life. We've looked at Saul's and Christ's deaths. How about yours?

● What will be said of you at your funeral? Be objective. Don't be overly hard on yourself, yet don't fudge on the facts. Consider these questions:

—What do you want on your tombstone?
—Saul said, "I have played the fool." What has been your role?
—Are you ready? Is your spiritual house in order?

 Digging Deeper

Suicide.

For some of you, the word is only a clinical one. For others, it hits all too close to home ... maybe someone you love has seen it as an answer, or maybe thoughts of suicide creep into your mind when life's pain seems too much to bear.

God has instilled in each of us a strong instinct to live. But sometimes so deep a sense of failure or loneliness or despair sets in that this desire to live is quelled by an even stronger desire to die.

Fortunately, potential suicide victims usually communicate their pain before acting, making suicide preventable if those near know the signals.

We've supplied you with a list of these warning signs to help alert you to the suicidal person's subtle cries for help.

1. Talking about suicide
2. A sudden change in personality
3. Deep depression
4. Physical symptoms: sleeplessness, loss of appetite, decreased sex drive, drastic weight loss, chronic exhaustion
5. Actual suicide attempts
6. Crisis situations: death of a loved one, failure at school, loss of a job, marital or home problems, a lengthy or terminal illness

If you recognize any of these signals in yourself or in someone you love, we urge you to get help.

- **Scripture**
  Scripture teaches two truths that encourage us to value our lives:
  1. Life is a gift from God to be cherished (Gen. 2:7, John 1:3).
  2. The One who gives life is the only one with authority to take it (1 Sam. 2:6, Ps. 31:15a).

- **Books**
  Duckworth, Marion. *Why Teens Are Killing Themselves.* San Bernardino, Calif.: Here's Life Publishers, 1987.
  Griest, John H., M.D., and James W. Jefferson, M.D. *Depression and Its Treatment.* Washington, D.C.: American Psychiatric Press, 1984.
  Grollman, Earl A. *Suicide—Prevention, Intervention, Postvention.* Kansas City, Mo.: Beacon Hill Press, 1971.
  Wright, H. Norman. *Crisis Counseling.* San Bernardino, Calif.: Here's Life Publishers, 1985.

- **Suicide Prevention and Intervention Organizations**
  The American Association of Suicidology, 2459 South Ash, Denver, Colorado 80222. Educational pamphlets are available, as well as guidelines for starting crisis facilities.
  National Institute of Mental Health, 5600 Fishers Lane, Rockville, Maryland 20857, Public Inquiries Branch, Room 15C-05. Information on suicide and related subjects is available.
  The Samaritans, 500 Commonwealth Avenue, Kenmore Square, Boston, Massachusetts 02215. Educational material is available.

- **Crisis Intervention Hotlines**
  If you feel like you've reached a point of desperation in your life, please realize that there is help from people who care. Many crisis intervention agencies are open 24 hours a day and can provide you with counseling and referrals. To get in touch with one of these agencies, please consult your local telephone book under "Crisis Intervention." There really is hope.

New King, New Throne, Same Lord
2 Samuel 1–5

In the four volumes of *Abraham Lincoln: The War Years,* Carl Sandburg discusses the darkest years of Lincoln's life, tracing the events that led to one of the saddest points in American history, Lincoln's assassination.

Following this section on Lincoln's death is a chapter whose title is drawn from an old woodsman's proverb: A tree is best measured when it's down. While Lincoln was still standing, his life couldn't properly be appraised. It took the felling of this great man for us to appreciate his solid-oak character.

So far in our study, we've been evaluating the knots and leaves of David's life. But today we want to measure the whole tree—from the tips of the roots to the very top branch—evaluating both his victories and his defeats.

I. Panoramic View of David's Life
From the yardstick of Psalm 78:70–71, we find a rough measurement of the seventy years of David's life.

> He also chose David His servant,
> And took him from the sheepfolds;
> From the care of the ewes with suckling lambs He brought
>   him,
> To shepherd Jacob His people,
> And Israel His inheritance.

During David's sapling years, his life was on an upshoot—he walked triumphantly with integrity in his heart. He never knew devastating failure, never experienced a defeat on the battlefield, never took a fatal excursion in the flesh. But his adulterous affair with Bathsheba bared the roots of David's sensuality, and his life began a downward slope toward tragedy.

II. From Fugitive to Monarch
Saul's death marked the end of David's fugitive days. It was finally time for him to be crowned king. Second Samuel 5:4–5 surveys his reign:

> David was thirty years old when he became king, and he reigned forty years. At Hebron he reigned over Judah seven years and six months, and in Jerusalem he reigned thirty-three years over all Israel and Judah.

A. King over Judah in Hebron. After lamenting Saul's death, David obeys God's instruction to go to Hebron (2 Sam. 2:1–2) to reign as Judah's king.

1. **A spiritual accomplishment.** In Jerusalem there were still some satellite kings—self-appointed men who had orbited around the kingship of Saul. However, David obeyed God in confining his rule to Judah, letting God handle the other kings in His own time and way. David didn't push the issue; he had learned to patiently trust in His will.
2. **Spiritual disappointments.** While in Hebron, David also made some decisions he lived to regret: he had a weakness for women, loving many and making many his wives.

> Sons were born to David at Hebron: his first-born was Amnon, by Ahinoam the Jezreelitess; and his second, Chileab, by Abigail the widow of Nabal the Carmelite; and the third, Absalom the son of Maacah, the daughter of Talmai, king of Geshur; and the fourth, Adonijah the son of Haggith; and the fifth, Shephatiah the son of Abital; and the sixth, Ithream, by David's wife Eglah. These were born to David at Hebron. (3:2–5)

Along with these, David had other wives and countless concubines. It was through these polygamous relationships that some of the gnarls in his character first made themselves known.

B. King over all Israel in Jerusalem. After reigning in Hebron, David moved his throne to Jerusalem (see 5:6–9). There he enjoyed a long reign, great power, and abundant blessing from God.

> And David became greater and greater, for the Lord God of hosts was with him. (2 Sam. 5:10)

Although God's hand was with David, he was still a man . . . still given to failure. His accomplishments in Jerusalem were mixed with some devastating disappointments.

1. **Accomplishments.**
   a. He expanded Israel's boundaries from 6,000 to 60,000 square miles.
   b. He established extensive trade routes to the entire known world.
   c. He unified the nation.
   d. He subdued Israel's enemies more completely than anyone had done since Joshua's time.
   e. He shaped a national interest in spiritual concerns.
2. **Disappointments.**
   a. He became so enamored with public pursuits that he lost control of his family. Again, he took more wives, had more children. David's immediate family, excluding

concubines and their children, consisted of nineteen sons and one daughter (1 Chron. 3:1–9). David had too many wives to attend to properly and too many children to discipline responsibly.[1]

> ### Managing the Home
> David was a king on the battlefield, but a pawn with his own family. Parents, do you put all your energies, all your wisdom, all your time into your own interests to the neglect of your children's needs for attention and discipline? What every child needs is firm discipline tempered with gentle, unconditional love (Prov. 3:12, 13:24, 22:15).[2]

b. He indulged himself in extravagant activities. Not only did David have numerous wives and concubines, but he also indulged himself in inappropriate seasons of leisure (2 Sam. 11:1). And he had an uncontrollable lust (11:4a). David's greatest fault was his quickness to embrace the passions of the flesh.

c. He became a victim of self-sufficiency and pride (24:1–3; 1 Chron. 21:1–7, 14).

> ### An Observation and a Warning
> It takes a certain temperament to be a dynamic leader—a certain charisma and winsomeness. But along with that type of personality comes a definite set of weaknesses for *silver, sloth, sex,* and *self.*
> If you're like David—a passionate, charismatic, live-life-to-the-hilt kind of person—be ready for Satan to attack you with these fiery arrows. Through prayer and self-discipline, you can toughen your heart to his assaults (see Matt. 26:41, Eph. 6:11–18).

III. Timeless and Priceless Truths to Live By

We've taken this time to measure David's life so that we could model his successes and avoid his failures. From David's experiences we

1. When Amnon raped his half sister, David's only response was anger (2 Sam. 13:21); when Adonijah exalted himself, saying, "I will be king," David never rebuked him or questioned his actions (1 Kings 1:5–6); and when Absalom rebelled, David fled (2 Sam. 15).

2. For additional guidance in raising children, see the study guide *You and Your Child*, co-authored by Ken Gire, from the Bible-teaching ministry of Charles R. Swindoll (Fullerton, Calif.: Insight for Living, 1986), pp. 27–43.

find two important truths that will help us become people after God's own heart.

A. No personal pursuit is more important than the cultivation of godliness into your family. This requires discipline, concern, courtesy, commitment, acceptance, and involvement.

B. No character trait needs more attention than integrity. This requires honesty, authenticity, standing alone, loyalty to principle, keeping one's word, and harmony between public and private life.

 Living Insights

Study One ▰▰▰▰▰▰▰▰▰▰▰▰▰▰▰▰▰▰▰▰▰▰▰▰▰▰▰▰

Since we've spent so much time examining the historical accounts of David's life, let's change our pace and take some time to look at the king's personal journal.

- Psalm 30 is the song David wrote to celebrate the dedication of his house in Jerusalem, an event that symbolized the establishment of his throne in Israel. Read the psalm carefully, and jot down David's feelings about God, enemies, prosperity, distress, and himself.

David's Thoughts from Psalm 30

God _____

_____

_____

Enemies _____

_____

_____

Prosperity _____

_____

_____

Distress _____

_____

_____

Continued on next page

Himself _____

_____

_____

🐎 *Living Insights*

Two timeless and priceless principles brought this lesson to a close. It is well worth our time to apply these truths to our lives.

● *No personal pursuit is more important than the cultivation of godliness into your family.* Looking at the specific areas below, evaluate yourself on a scale of 1 to 5 (5 meaning you're doing very well).

____ Discipline   ____ Commitment

____ Concern   ____ Acceptance

____ Courtesy   ____ Involvement

Where did you score lowest? Write out some steps you can take to begin working on that area today.

_____

_____

_____

_____

● *No character trait needs more attention than integrity.* Look at the following areas and rate yourself as you did above.

____ Honesty   ____ Loyalty to Principle

____ Authenticity   ____ Keeping Your Word

____ Standing Alone   ____ Public/Private Harmony

Which area needs the most improvement? Think through a strategy for improvement, and write down your thoughts.

_____

_____

_____

_____

David and the Ark
2 Samuel 6

At the mention of David's name, a myriad of pictures floods our minds.

David the shepherd boy, playing his harp in the pastures. David the warrior, slaying Goliath with the whistling fling of a stone. David the adulterer, feasting his lust on Bathsheba. David the father, weeping over the death of his son Absalom.

Although these cameos breathe life into our understanding of David, none of them are highlighted in the New Testament. Only one description has lingered throughout the centuries to epitaph his life: David, the man after God's own heart (see Acts 13:22).

One of the things that linked his heart to God's was that he took God seriously. Although he sometimes failed, he purposed to obey not only God's principles but His precepts—the specific, detailed instructions God has given His children.[1]

In this study, David restores the ark of the covenant to Israel. Once again he proves himself committed to obeying the Lord . . . once again, a man whose life pulsed to the heartbeat of God.

I. Setting the Scene

Israel had become spiritually malnourished under Saul's reign (see 1 Chron. 13:3). The tabernacle had deteriorated, its furnishings had been scattered, the worship itself had become virtually meaningless. Since God's presence was associated with the tabernacle furnishings, the people of Israel no longer felt His nearness. As Israel's new king, David wanted to reestablish the center of worship—to renew his people's fear of God and fatten their spiritual fervor.

II. Transporting the Ark

Reestablishing tabernacle worship meant gathering the scattered articles of furniture and arranging them according to the order God gave in Exodus 25–27. The most important piece of tabernacle furniture was the ark of the covenant—the very place where God met His people.

A. The ark.

1. **Description.** The ark was a chest made of acacia wood, gold-plated inside and out, and rimmed with a border of gold. It was 3¾ feet long, 2½ feet wide, and 2¼ feet high. Its pure gold lid—the mercy seat—held two cherubs of

---

1. Precepts give specific, detailed instruction; principles give general directions. For example, a sign that reads 35 MPH gives a precept; but a sign that reads Drive Carefully gives a principle.

hammered gold, with wings outstretched over the cover. The ark held only three objects: a golden jar containing manna, Aaron's rod, and the Ten Commandments (Heb. 9:4).

The Holy Place

Even before the cross, worship was highly symbolic, related to types and pictures. When the Israelites looked at the ark, they saw more than a box made of acacia wood and gold. They saw holiness . . . the very glory of God.

Although there is no longer a tabernacle, an ark of the covenant, or a holy of holies, God's presence is still found in a valuable vessel. This vessel—lined with the priceless gold of forgiveness—is every believer's heart (2 Cor. 6:16).

---

2. **Displacement.** As we pick up the account in 2 Samuel 6, the ark rests in the home of Abinadab (vv. 2–3), located on a hill in Baale-judah, about ten miles west of Jerusalem.[2]
3. **Directions.** God's instructions on how the ark was to be carried were explicit. Gold rings were fixed at the corners of both long sides of the ark, and gold-plated poles were to be slipped through the rings so the ark could be carried without being touched. The ark was to be carried only by Levites (Num. 3:6–10).

B. The death. In his zeal to bring the ark to Jerusalem, David overlooked God's instructions on how to transport it, bringing it instead on the wheels of haste and convenience.

> And they placed the ark of God on a new cart that they might bring it from the house of Abinadab which was on the hill; and Uzzah and Ahio, the sons of Abinadab, were leading the new cart. . . . But when they came to the threshing floor of Nacon, Uzzah reached out toward the ark of God and took hold of it, for the oxen nearly upset it. (2 Sam. 6:3, 6)

Instead of being carried on the shoulders of Levites, the ark was carried on a cart. And instead of revering the ark, Uzzah touched

---

2. While Eli was judge over Israel, the Philistines captured the ark from the tabernacle (1 Sam. 5). But God sent a plague upon them, so they returned it to Beth-shemesh. The men of Beth-shemesh, however, committed sacrilege when they looked into the ark, and God struck down 50,070 of their men (1 Sam. 6). Because of this tragedy, the survivors of Beth-shemesh asked the men of Kiriath-jearim to take the ark away, and they brought it to the house of Abinadab.

it, desecrating its holiness.[3] Clearly, David had overlooked the details of God's plan—details so important to God that He took Uzzah's life.

> And the anger of the Lord burned against Uzzah, and
> God struck him down there for his irreverence; and
> he died there by the ark of God. (v. 7)

As Uzzah's body lay alongside the ark, David's anger burned against God, until a fear of the Lord gripped his raging heart and turned him back.

> And David became angry because of the Lord's out-
> burst against Uzzah. . . . So David was afraid of the
> Lord that day; and he said, "How can the ark of the
> Lord come to me?" (vv. 8a, 9)

David wasn't perfect. But he *was* sensitive to sin. He admitted his wrong and began to take God seriously. Humbly, he refused to move the ark to Jerusalem and took it to the house of Obed-edom instead (vv. 10–11).

C. The change. During the three months the ark was with Obed-edom, David watched the blessing it brought to his home, which made David anxious to bring the ark to his city.

> Now it was told King David, saying, "The Lord has
> blessed the house of Obed-edom and all that belongs
> to him, on account of the ark of God." And David
> went and brought up the ark of God from the house
> of Obed-edom into the city of David with gladness.
> (v. 12)

What happened to make David change his mind about bringing the ark to Jerusalem? A parallel passage, 1 Chronicles 15:11–15, gives us some behind-the-scenes information. Following Uzzah's tragic death, David did his homework and, with the help of the Levites and priests, discovered the proper way to transport the ark. As David speaks to the Levites, notice his humble and honest assessment of his sin against God.

> "Because you did not carry it at the first, the Lord our
> God made an outburst on us, for we did not seek
> Him according to the ordinance." (v. 13)

David not only admitted his wrong, the next time around he made it right.

---

3. "The punishment of Uzzah has often been objected to as excessive, especially as his intention was good; but the majesty of the Holy One was symbolized by the ark. It was necessary to teach the Israelites the infinite holiness of God, sometimes by 'terrible acts'." From *The Eerdmans Bible Commentary,* 3d ed., ed. D. Guthrie and J. A. Motyer (Grand Rapids, Mich.: William B. Eerdmans Publishing Co., 1987. © 1970 Inter-Varsity Press, London), p. 305.

And the sons of the Levites carried the ark of God on their shoulders, with the poles thereon as Moses had commanded according to the word of the Lord. (v. 15)

Rings and Poles

When it comes to obeying God, it's the details—the rings and poles—that snag us. Either we don't want to go to the trouble of getting the poles, or we don't want to carry them upon our shoulders. So we grab a cart, rewrite the rules, and do it our own way.

When you disobey God's precepts, He may not strike you dead like He did Uzzah, but His grief runs just as deep.

Are there some rings and poles you've been ignoring? Claiming every source of income at tax time . . . being kind to someone else's difficult child . . . honoring the authorities in your life?

Being a person after God's heart means caring about what He cares about, grieving over what grieves Him, and being willing to do His will, His way.

III. Celebrating the Lord

Some might think that following every detail of God's law would make you unbending, stern. But this wasn't the case with David. When the ark finally reached Jerusalem, David celebrated in a way that was anything but rigid.

A. David's dance.

> And David was dancing before the Lord with all his might, and David was wearing a linen ephod. So David and all the house of Israel were bringing up the ark of the Lord with shouting and the sound of the trumpet. (2 Sam. 6:14–15)[4]

W. Phillip Keller comments on David's celebration dance:

> For David, it was much more than a religious rite. It was the release from his remorse; the restoration of his joy in the Lord after profound repentance; the liberation of his whole person from fear of having offended the Almighty.
>
> In jubilation and pure adoration he began to leap and bound into the air with exhilaration. His poetic

---

4. During the celebration, David composed one of his most magnificent psalms (see 1 Chron. 16:7–36). Few others match this one for the honor, glory, power, and majesty poured out upon God.

soul and artistic nature had to find full expression
of gratitude in acknowledging that God, very God,
deigned once more to come and dwell among His
people.[5]

B. Michal's response. Now in obedience to God, David was
free. And whenever you're truly free, someone in the bondage
of disobedience will envy your freedom—and will try to still
your dance. David's wet blanket was his own wife Michal.

Then it happened as the ark of the Lord came into
the city of David that Michal the daughter of Saul
looked out of the window and saw King David leaping
and dancing before the Lord; and she despised him
in her heart.... When David returned to bless his
household, Michal the daughter of Saul came out to
meet David and said, "How the king of Israel distinguished himself today! He uncovered himself today
in the eyes of his servants' maids as one of the foolish
ones shamelessly uncovers himself!" (vv. 16, 20)

Michal's sarcastic, jealous jabs didn't sink David's joy. Caring
more about God's opinion than Michal's, he defended his right
to celebrate before his Lord.

So David said to Michal, "It was before the Lord, who
chose me above your father and above all his house,
to appoint me ruler over the people of the Lord, over
Israel; therefore I will celebrate before the Lord. And
I will be more lightly esteemed than this and will be
humble in my own eyes, but with the maids of whom
you have spoken, with them I will be distinguished."
(vv. 21–22)

As a consequence of her hatred toward David, Michal bore no
children her whole life (v. 23). To a Jewish woman, the greatest
curse was a barren womb.

IV. A Lesson Learned

From David's episode with the ark, we learn that *the better you know
where you stand with the Lord, the freer you can be.* David wasn't
free before God until he understood and obeyed His precepts about
the ark. But once he did, God filled his sagging, repentant spirit with
exuberance and joy. Dietrich Bonhoeffer capsulizes the relevance of
this passage to our lives.

But to deviate from the truth for the sake of some prospect of hope of our own can never be wise, however
slight that deviation may be. It is not our judgement of

5. W. Phillip Keller, *David: The Shepherd King* (Waco, Tex.: Word Books, 1986), vol. 2, p. 55.

the situation which can show us what is wise, but only the truth of the Word of God. Here alone lies the promise of God's faithfulness and help. It will always be true that the wisest course for the disciple is always to abide solely by the Word of God in all simplicity.[6]

A person after God's heart . . . someone committed to obeying every part of His Word. Are you that person?

 Living Insights

Study One ▬▬▬▬▬▬▬▬▬▬▬▬▬▬▬▬▬▬▬

The ark described in 2 Samuel 6 was a symbol of the very presence of God. It represented His holiness and His mercy toward men. Let's study the ark in a little more depth.

- Gather a set of helps for your study on the ark of the covenant. You may want a Bible dictionary, a Bible encyclopedia, or a book that describes Bible customs. Look up the ark of the covenant and write down what you find in the following chart.

The Ark of the Covenant	
Sources	Observations

6. Dietrich Bonhoeffer, as quoted in *A Long Obedience in the Same Direction,* by Eugene H. Peterson (Downers Grove, Ill.: InterVarsity Press, 1980), p. 32.

Living Insights

Acts 13:22 gives us the Lord's description of David: " ' "I have found David the son of Jesse, a man after My heart, who will do all My will." ' " This is perhaps the finest compliment anyone could ever receive. Could God say this of you? Use the following questions to examine your heart, answering honestly and openly.

● What does it mean to have a heart for God?

_____

_____

_____

_____

● Are there precepts from God you aren't taking seriously?

_____

_____

_____

_____

● What are some areas of freedom in your life? What are some areas of bondage?

_____

_____

_____

_____

● What are one or two things you've learned from the questions above? How will you apply them?

_____

_____

_____

_____

When God Says No

2 Samuel 7

Ready on the tongue of every parent is the bread-and-butter word *no*. At any moment, it may need to stop a toddler about to touch a hot stove, scale the living room couch, or swallow a handful of marbles.

But *no* isn't always a reprimand given to stop a child from harm. Often it is the answer to an innocuous request or an innocent plan—because the parent has something better in mind for the child.

Likewise, God occasionally tells His children no. And while He usually says no to stop us from sinning, sometimes He says no to our plans and dreams to save our energies for a greater cause.

The hard thing about these kinds of nos is that the *why* is often left a mystery. It seems that God is giving us the enigmatic parental answer that clangs in the ear of every child: "Just because I said so."

Today we will look at a time when God stamped the box of David's dreams with a bold, black NO. And we'll see how David handled it—whether David ran *from* God in disillusionment or *to* Him in contentment and trust.

I. A Peaceful Interlude

So far, David's life has been like a great symphony that flows from one passionate movement to another. But in 2 Samuel 7, it pauses to play a tranquil strain. Finally, the courageous warrior is allowed to rest.

A. Domestic peace. Etched over the fireplace of David's home was the word *Shalom.*[1] The fire crackled the sounds of peace and well-being.

B. National rest. There were no Philistines to contend with ... no strategies to be made. There were no blaspheming giants ... no rumbling chariot wheels (v. 1b).

C. Personal desire. Nestled in his beautiful cedar house, David began to entertain a dream. Wanting only to bring God glory, he decides to build a temple to house the ark. David confides in his counselor, the prophet Nathan.

> "See now, I dwell in a house of cedar, but the ark of
> God dwells within tent curtains." (v. 2)

Nathan assures him that his plan is aligned with God's will.

> And Nathan said to the king, "Go, do all that is in
> your mind, for the Lord is with you." (v. 3)

But the prophet speaks too soon, putting words into God's mouth.

---

1. *Shalom* is the Hebrew word for "peace."

Our Dreams and God's Will

It's often during the quiet interludes of our lives—times when we slow down enough to reflect on our past and find new direction, new hope for our future—that we seize new dreams.

Yet, just because we've pulled back from the rat race doesn't mean that every dream is from God. Not even admirable dreams—even though God's people may affirm their value. David may have gotten the go-ahead from Nathan, but the final word came from God. Only He knows His plan for our lives.

II. A Divine Response

God responds to David's plan with a gracious refusal and a prophetic word.

A. Refusal of the request.

And it came about the same night, that the word of God came to Nathan, saying, "Go and tell David My servant, 'Thus says the Lord, "You shall not build a house for Me to dwell in." ' " (1 Chron. 17:3–4; see also 2 Sam. 7:4–7)

God's refusal wasn't a rejection, but a redirection. He had a different dream for David.

B. Plans for the future.
After refusing David's request, God affirms him, assuring David that He has given him something significant to do. Speaking through Nathan, God tells David:

" ' "I took you from the pasture, from following the sheep, that you should be ruler over My people Israel. And I have been with you wherever you have gone and have cut off all your enemies from before you; and I will make you a great name, like the names of the great men who are on the earth. I will also appoint a place for My people Israel and will plant them, that they may live in their own place and not be disturbed again, nor will the wicked afflict them any more as formerly, even from the day that I commanded judges to be over My people Israel; and I will give you rest from all your enemies. The Lord also declares to you that the Lord will make a house for you." ' " (2 Sam. 7:8b–11)

God not only assures David of His plan for his life, but He also patches his burst bubble with the promise that the temple he dreamed of would one day be built by his own son.

" ' "When your days are complete and you lie down with your fathers, I will raise up your descendant after you, who will come forth from you, and I will establish his kingdom. He shall build a house for My name, and I will establish the throne of his kingdom forever." ' " (vv. 12–13)

A Better Plan

God didn't gift David as a builder, but as a soldier and king. There was nothing wrong with David's dream. His motives were pure; his intentions, pleasing to God. But he wasn't the right man to carry out the plan; God wanted a man of peace to build His temple.

Has God ever said no to one of your dreams—going to the mission field . . . marrying a certain person who walked close to God? This kind of mysterious no is hard to handle. But if you believe that God really loves you, really wants what's best for you—if you trust Him with your life—He will show you the better plan He has for you.

Where do you run when God tells you no? To the arms of disillusionment—or to the embrace of God?

III. A Triumphant Prayer

When God told David no, David ran to Him and sat at His feet—thankful, tenderhearted, trusting (2 Sam. 7:18a).

A. Grateful questions. Like a humbled child, David expresses his trust through a series of questions.

"Who am I, O Lord God, and what is my house, that Thou hast brought me this far? And yet this was insignificant in Thine eyes, O Lord God, for Thou hast spoken also of the house of Thy servant concerning the distant future. And this is the custom of man, O Lord God. And again what more can David say to Thee? For Thou knowest Thy servant, O Lord God!" (vv. 18b–20)

David rested in the fact that God knew and understood him fully.

B. Insightful declarations. Still sitting in God's presence, David showers the Lord with a fragrant sacrifice of praise and faith.

"For this reason Thou art great, O Lord God; for there is none like Thee, and there is no God besides Thee. . . . Now therefore, O Lord God, the word that Thou hast spoken concerning Thy servant and his house, confirm it forever, and do as Thou has spoken, that Thy

name may be magnified forever....And now, O Lord
God, Thou art God, and Thy words are truth, and
Thou hast promised this good thing to Thy servant.
Now therefore, may it please Thee to bless the house
of Thy servant, that it may continue forever before
Thee. For Thou, O Lord God, hast spoken; and with
Thy blessing may the house of Thy servant be blessed
forever." (vv. 22a, 25–26a, 28–29)

IV. Two Lasting Applications

David's response to God's no was godly, gracious, full of trust. Perhaps louder than the words he spoke is the sound of his heart beating in sync with God's. In our efforts to become people after God's heart, we should observe two lasting truths.

A. When God says no, He has a better way. He never intends to frustrate or disillusion us when He says no to one of our dreams. He only wants to show us something better.

B. When God says no, our best reaction is humility and cooperation. Like David, who trusted God even when He took away his dream, we need to humbly submit to His will for us.

> *"Children of the Heavenly Father"*
> Though He giveth or He taketh,
> God His children ne'er forsaketh;
> His the loving purpose solely
> To preserve them pure and holy.[2]

Continued on next page

2. Carolina Sandell Berg, "Children of the Heavenly Father," trans. Ernst W. Olson, in *The Hymnal for Worship & Celebration* (Waco, Tex.: Word Music, 1986), no. 44.

Living Insights

David's desire to build the temple is a picture of his love for God. Our study of 2 Samuel 7 has taught us much about David's dream. Let's take some time now to study a parallel passage—1 Chronicles 17—to get another perspective.

- In the following charts, record observations about the story that are identical in both books. Then write down additional information unique to either 2 Samuel 7 or 1 Chronicles 17.

David's Temple

Identical Observations

Observations Unique to 2 Samuel 7

```
┌─────────────────────────────────────────────────────┐
│         Observations Unique to 1 Chronicles 17        │
├─────────────────────────────────────────────────────┤
│                                                       │
│                                                       │
│                                                       │
│                                                       │
│                                                       │
│                                                       │
│                                                       │
│                                                       │
│                                                       │
└─────────────────────────────────────────────────────┘
```

 Living Insights

Study Two ━━

Perhaps this lesson introduced you to a new truth. Maybe you didn't know that sometimes God says no to redirect and not punish us. Let's discuss this further.

● Can you look back to a time when God said no to you? Was it an answer that was not necessarily meant as discipline or rejection? Have you carried needless guilt with you because you felt you did something wrong?

● How are you at handling broken dreams? What has been your strategy in the past? Have you found that God provides a better way? Have you seen God raise up someone else to see your plan to fruition? Have you been cooperative and supportive? What has God taught you through these experiences?

Grace in a Barren Place
2 Samuel 9

A dancer's pirouette . . . people who carry themselves with charm and poise . . . a prayer given before a meal . . . music's most delicate notes. Each wears the tag *grace.*

But of all that this word identifies, its most significant meaning lies deep in the person of God.

Grace is God snatching us from a barren place—from a dry, desolate life of sin—and setting us to eat from the bounty of His table. It is undeserved and unrepayable . . . it is free.

In this lesson, we come to one of Scripture's richest illustrations of grace. Patterning his heart after God's by extending acceptance and mercy, David showers a shriveled soul with a refreshing rain of grace.

I. An Example of Grace
Still enjoying a peaceful interlude, David begins to reflect on promises he made to Saul and Jonathan before he was crowned king.

A. Promises made. In Eastern dynasties, when a new king took over it was common for him to kill every member of his predecessor's family. When Jonathan first heard that David would succeed his father to the throne, he asked him to spare his descendants. So David extended a hand of grace, making a covenant with Jonathan (1 Sam. 20:13–16). Saul, too, asked that David protect his family. And to him David vowed amnesty also (24:21–22).

B. A question asked. As the solemn words of David's vows echo in his mind, he asks Saul's servant Ziba:

"Is there not yet anyone of the house of Saul to whom I may show the kindness of God?" (2 Sam. 9:3a)

Notice that David asks for *anyone.* Not anyone worthy or anyone qualified—but is there anyone? David's kindness is unconditional and free.

C. An answer given.

And Ziba said to the king, "There is still a son of Jonathan who is crippled in both feet." (v. 3b)

Between the lines of Ziba's answer lies some cautious counsel. "You'd better think twice before you do this, David. This guy's not very kingly; he doesn't really fit the surroundings. He's crippled, David . . . on crutches."

D. A cripple sought. But, like grace, David isn't picky. He is intent on showing mercy to any of Jonathan's descendants, no matter how handicapped they might be.

So the king said to him, "Where is he?" And Ziba said
to the king, "Behold, he is in the house of Machir the
son of Ammiel in Lo-debar." (v. 4)

Lo-debar means "no pasture." He lived in the barren fields of
Palestine, where he was hiding from David's kingly sword.

1. **An explanation.** Second Samuel 4:4 tells us the tragic way
   Jonathan's son became crippled.

   Now Jonathan, Saul's son, had a son crippled in
   his feet. He was five years old when the report
   of Saul and Jonathan came from Jezreel, and his
   nurse took him up and fled. And it happened that
   in her hurry to flee, he fell and became lame.
   And his name was Mephibosheth.[1]

2. **Mephibosheth taken.** Picture it. Mephibosheth, hiding in
   fear of his life, is taken from his barren land by David's men
   (9:5). Mephibosheth's life must have flashed across his mind
   in a frightened blur.

   And Mephibosheth, the son of Jonathan the son of
   Saul, came to David and fell on his face and pros-
   trated himself. And David said, "Mephibosheth."
   And he said, "Here is your servant!" (v. 6)

II. The Result of Grace

As David tells Mephibosheth of his promise to his father, Mephibosheth's festering fear is salved with words of grace.

And David said to him, "Do not fear, for I will surely show
kindness to you for the sake of your father Jonathan, and
will restore to you all the land of your grandfather Saul;
and you shall eat at my table regularly." Again he pros-
trated himself and said, "What is your servant, that you
should regard a dead dog like me?" Then the king called
Saul's servant Ziba, and said to him, "All that belonged
to Saul and to all his house I have given to your master's
grandson. And you and your sons and your servants shall
cultivate the land for him, and you shall bring in the
produce so that your master's grandson may have food;
nevertheless Mephibosheth your master's grandson shall
eat at my table regularly." (vv. 7–10a)

Mephibosheth is plucked from the wastelands to live in the king's
palace. Once clothed in the rags of obscurity and fear, he is now
draped in the garments of honor and security.

---

1. The name Mephibosheth means "one who scatters shame." The root words convey the idea
of one who is despised or held in contempt—a laughingstock, a shameful thing . . . humiliation.

III. Application by Analogy

This scene from David's life gifts us with a priceless set of analogies between the crippled Mephibosheth and the king, analogies that exemplify the relationship between the sinner and the Lord.

A. Mephibosheth once enjoyed fellowship with his father, and so did man with his Creator in the Garden of Eden. Just as Adam walked with the sovereign God in the cool of the evening, so, having been part of the royal family, Mephibosheth knew what it was like to live face-to-face with a king.

B. When disaster and fear came, the nurse fled and Mephibosheth suffered a fall that left him crippled. When temptation came, man fell from holiness and became spiritually handicapped.

C. Out of love for Jonathan, David demonstrated grace to his crippled son. So God, out of love for His Son Jesus, shows His love to us.

D. Mephibosheth had nothing, deserved nothing, and, in fact, didn't even try to win the king's favor. We, too, are completely undeserving of God's grace and cannot win His favor by any merit of our own (Eph. 2:8–9).

E. David took Mephibosheth from a barren place and restored him to a place of honor. God has also taken us from our spiritual desolation and made us heirs with the King.

F. David adopted Mephibosheth into his family, and he became the king's son. God has adopted us into His family and made us His children (Eph. 1:5, 1 John 3:1).

G. Mephibosheth's crippled limp was a constant reminder of grace. So we, with the limp of sin, are continually reminded that God in His mercy has not dealt with us according to our sins (Ps. 103:10–14).

H. When Mephibosheth sat down at the royal table, he was treated just like one of the king's sons. Likewise, when we enter into God's presence, we will sit at His table as equal recipients of His love.

Grace in a Barren Place

I was that Mephibosheth
Crippled by my twisted pride and
    hiding from You in a barren place
        where You could not find me
        where You would not give me what I de-
            served

98

But somehow You found me and
I don't understand why but You
    gave me what I *do not* deserve
You not only spared my desolate life but
    You made it bountiful
And here at Your table
I will thank You my
    King

—Julie Martin

 Living Insights

Study One

Finding illustrations of God's grace from the Scriptures is easy. Many good examples come to mind almost immediately. However, did you think of Mephibosheth? He may be unfamiliar, but he sure illustrates the point!

- In order to get a better handle on this true story, let's take some time to paraphrase 2 Samuel 9. As you know, paraphrasing is taking a passage of Scripture and rewriting it in your own words. In doing so, you are able to expand on the meanings and emotions that can be discovered beneath the words of the text. This is such a wonderful story of God's grace . . . take your time and enjoy it.

_____

_____

_____

_____

_____

_____

_____

_____

_____

_____

Continued on next page

_____

_____

_____

_____

_____

_____

_____

_____

_____

_____

_____

_____

_____

_____

_____

_____

 Living Insights

Study Two ▬▬▬▬▬▬▬▬▬▬▬▬▬▬▬▬▬▬▬▬▬▬▬▬

Mephibosheth . . . what a beautiful picture of God's grace. A lesson of this nature sparks true worship in a believer's heart. God's grace is matchless. We have so much to be thankful for.

- Let's use today's Living Insights to worship God. You may choose to do this alone or with close friends or family. Your worship may include some of the following ideas, or it may be entirely different! Enjoy this time of response to God.

—Write God a letter, thanking Him for His grace in your life.
—Sing your worship to God. Offer Him choruses and hymns of praise.
—If you're with others, share items of praise and thanksgiving.
—Take a walk and reflect on God's grace while enjoying His creation.

The Case of the Open Window Shade

2 Samuel 11

When the Holy Spirit painted the portraits of Scripture's heroes, He was an artist of pure realism—refusing to brush with high-gloss colors the darker sides of their lives.

As we've studied the biblical portrait of David's life, we've seen both the bright hues of faith and the somber colors of failure. But today we will look at the blackest part of the picture—David's encounter with Bathsheba.

Our purpose for this lesson is not to shake our fingers at David's shame, but to humbly heed the counsel of 1 Corinthians 10:12,

Let him who thinks he stands take heed lest he fall.

I. A Black Backdrop

At the time of his fall into sin, David was around fifty years old and had been Israel's king for about two decades. He had distinguished himself as a gifted musician, a valiant warrior, a man of God. Yet, even with this impressive résumé, he had his faults. Like a seawall standing against the constant barrage of the churning sea, in a weak moment, he crumbled. We can trace his fall to three weaknesses.

A. Lust. Second Samuel 5:12–13 reveals this crack in David's character.

And David realized that the Lord had established him as king over Israel, and that He had exalted his kingdom for the sake of His people Israel. Meanwhile David took more concubines and wives from Jerusalem, after he came from Hebron; and more sons and daughters were born to David.

From the way these verses were written, we could get the idea that David's polygamy was acceptable. But it directly violated the precepts God gave in Deuteronomy 17:

"You shall surely set a king over you whom the Lord your God chooses, one from among your countrymen you shall set as king over yourselves. . . . *Neither shall he multiply wives for himself, lest his heart turn away.*"
(vv. 15a, 17a, emphasis added)

As David's harem grew, so did his lust. Brick by falling brick, the wall of his integrity was crumbled by the crashing waves of passion.

B. Complacency. David's career was at an all-time high. Fresh from a series of victories in battle, he had reached the peak of public admiration. He enjoyed an endless supply of money, power, and fame. Never are we more vulnerable than when we have it all, and David was no exception.

C. Indulgence. Perhaps David placed too much stock in his track record; he began to sit back in his easy chair and let others tend to his kingly responsibilities.

> Then it happened in the spring, at the time when kings go out to battle, that David sent Joab and his servants with him and all Israel, and they destroyed the sons of Ammon and besieged Rabbah. But David stayed at Jerusalem. (2 Sam. 11:1)

While David's men were in battle, he was home in bed, cushioned by royal comforts (v. 2a).

— A Thought to Consider —

Our greatest battles don't come when we're out working hard, they come when we have time on our hands. It's in the warm springtime when we're yawning and stretching with boredom that we make those fateful decisions that end up haunting us.

II. A Sensuous Scene

Black tragedy shrouded the sky of that lazy spring evening.

A. A lurid thought. It all began with a look.

> Now when evening came David arose from his bed and walked around on the roof of the king's house, and from the roof he saw a woman bathing; and the woman was very beautiful in appearance. (v. 2)

One look at this beautiful woman and David's lust was enflamed. Dietrich Bonhoeffer illuminates the struggle we have with impure desires.

> In our members there is a slumbering inclination towards desire which is both sudden and fierce. With irresistible power desire seizes mastery over the flesh. All at once a secret, smouldering fire is kindled. The flesh burns and is in flames. It makes no difference whether it is sexual desire, or ambition, or vanity, or desire for revenge, or love of fame and power, or greed for money, or, finally, that strange desire for the beauty of the world, of nature. Joy in God is ... extinguished in us and we seek all our joy in the creature. At this moment God is quite unreal to us, he loses all reality, and only desire for the

creature is real; the only reality is the devil. Satan does not here fill us with hatred of God, but with forgetfulness of God. . . . The lust thus aroused envelops the mind and will of man in deepest darkness. The powers of clear discrimination and of decision are taken from us. . . .

It is here that everything within me rises up against the Word of God. . . .

Therefore the Bible teaches us in times of temptation in the flesh to *flee:* 'Flee fornication' (I Cor. 6.18)—'from idolatry' (I Cor. 10.14)—'youthful lusts' (II Tim. 2.22)—'the lust of the world' (II Pet. 1.4). There is no resistance to Satan other than flight. Every struggle against lust in one's own strength is doomed to failure.[1]

As David gazed upon the woman, he forgot about his devotion to God. Instead of fleeing his lusts, he sought to fulfill them.

So David sent and inquired about the woman. And one said, "Is this not Bathsheba, the daughter of Eliam, the wife of Uriah the Hittite?" And David sent messengers and took her. (vv. 3–4a)

B. A lustful act. Scripture's description of the encounter is brief but complete. Notice that there appears to be neither struggle nor surprise on Bathsheba's part.

And when she came to him, he lay with her; and when she had purified herself from her uncleanness, she returned to her house. (v. 4b)

A Word to Women

Although David instigated the encounter with Bathsheba, Bathsheba wasn't a blameless victim. She didn't draw her shades; as she drew her bath, she poured temptation in David's path.

Women, your physical appearance can be the nemesis of a man. Are the clothes you wear snares to the men around you? Or do they cover you in modesty and purity?

C. A lingering result. No doubt the stolen water of David and Bathsheba's sin was sweet, but the consequences soon turned it bitter—and the taste lingered on their lips for a lifetime.

And the woman conceived; and she sent and told David, and said, "I am pregnant." (v. 5)

---

1. Dietrich Bonhoeffer, *Temptation* (1955; reprint, London, England: SCM Press, 1964), pp. 33–34.

Satan never tells the heavy drinker, "Tomorrow there'll be a hangover." He never warns the drug user, "Be sure not to overdose." He never tells the adulterer, "Pregnancy is a real possibility—and so is disease."

He lures you with the alcohol, the drugs, the beautiful body. But when it's time for you to reap the consequences, he's gone.

When you're in the heat of temptation, remember how real the consequences of your sin can be—they can change the course of your life forever.

III. A Panic Plan

Instead of facing his sin and confessing it before God and his counselors, David panicked and chose to develop a cover-up plan—trading his integrity for hypocrisy and deceit.

A. Deception and hypocrisy. David's plan was to bring Bathsheba's husband Uriah back from battle so that he would lie with his wife and assume that she had conceived *his* child.

> Then David sent to Joab, saying, "Send me Uriah the Hittite." So Joab sent Uriah to David. When Uriah came to him, David asked concerning the welfare of Joab and the people and the state of the war. (vv. 6–7)

David's questions reeked with hypocrisy. He didn't care about Joab or the war. He was only keeping up appearances.

> Then David said to Uriah, "Go down to your house, and wash your feet." And Uriah went out of the king's house, and a present from the king was sent out after him. (v. 8)

Sending Uriah a gift was merely another ploy from David's deceitful hands. Nevertheless, David's efforts to get Uriah home to his wife didn't work.

> But Uriah slept at the door of the king's house with all the servants of his lord, and did not go down to his house. Now when they told David, saying, "Uriah did not go down to his house," David said to Uriah, "Have you not come from a journey? Why did you not go down to your house?" (vv. 9–10)

Uriah's response to David's question must have pricked David's conscience with guilt.

> And Uriah said to David, "The ark and Israel and Judah are staying in temporary shelters, and my lord Joab and the servants of my lord are camping in the

open field. Shall I then go to my house to eat and to drink and to lie with my wife? By your life and the life of your soul, I will not do this thing." (v. 11)

David, the commander in chief, was rebuked by the integrity of a soldier—a man who was completely committed to the nation, to his king, and to the Lord. As a last attempt at getting Uriah to go home to his wife, David wined and dined him until he was drunk. But still, Uriah wouldn't go home (v. 13).

B. Violence and murder. What had happened to turn David—a man of God—into a deceitful hypocrite? Paid with the wages of lust, he had become spiritually schizophrenic. And his "harmless" cover-up plan turned into cold-blooded murder. By way of Uriah, David sent Joab a message to put Uriah on the front battle lines and abandon him there; David knew he would surely be killed (vv. 14–15). As the result of David's plan, not only did Uriah die, but a number of other innocent soldiers as well (v. 24).

Playing with Fire

Playing with sin is playing with fire. If you don't snuff out temptation when it first sparks in your mind, the fire may burn out of control.

What started as a lustful thought in David's mind spread to adultery, which spread to deception, which culminated in murder.

We urge you to take temptation seriously. Stop sin before it ever starts. And if there's already a blaze of sin charring your life, it's not too late to turn from your wrong and experience the cool, quenching water of the Spirit's forgiveness (1 John 1:9, Ps. 32:5).

IV. A Complete Cover-Up

A. Before the troops. When the word of Uriah's death reached David, he pretended to know nothing about it, giving a hypocritical you-win-some-you-lose-some response.

Then David said to the messenger, "Thus you shall say to Joab, 'Do not let this thing displease you, for the sword devours one as well as another; make your battle against the city stronger and overthrow it;' and so encourage him." (2 Sam. 11:25)

B. Before the nation. On the surface, everything seemed perfectly normal—a burial, days of mourning, flowers, chants. Then, when Bathsheba was through grieving,

David sent and brought her to his house and she became his wife; then she bore him a son. (v. 27b)

C. But not before God. Although David had completely deceived the nation, he hadn't covered up his sin in God's eyes.

> But the thing that David had done was evil in the sight of the Lord. (v. 27c)

Not once had David sought God's counsel or forgiveness. He had maintained his integrity in the eyes of the people, he could now enjoy Bathsheba as his wife . . . but his fellowship with God was broken.

"Take Heed . . ."

As we've looked at this blackest part of David's portrait, we've seen that even the godly can fall.

If you think you're standing pure before God, take heed. Unless you lean on God's strength, you might stumble.

Won't you cling to the Lord Jesus—the only one who "is able to keep you from stumbling, and to make you stand in the presence of His glory blameless with great joy" (Jude 24)?

 Living Insights

Study One ▪▪▪▪▪▪▪▪▪▪▪▪▪▪▪▪▪

"The one who commits adultery with a woman is lacking sense; / He who would destroy himself does it" (Prov. 6:32). David's son Solomon made this powerful comment in his book of Proverbs.

- Many people feel Christians overreact when it comes to sexual sin. But God's Word is quite clear about it. Let's concentrate our efforts in just one book of the Bible—the book of Proverbs. Read through the references below, and jot down thoughts you feel would be helpful in dealing with a person involved in or contemplating sexual sin.

Proverbs 5

Proverbs 6:23–35

Proverbs 7

Continued on next page

Living Insights

In our previous study we did some research on sexual immorality. Let's make what we've learned practical.

- Based on what you discovered in Study One, what are your convictions regarding sexual immorality? Take this time to write a letter expressing your thoughts on this issue. You may want to address it to someone in your life who is struggling with this matter or to a young Christian who is not yet fully grounded in God's Word. You may not choose to mail the letter; the importance of this exercise is to clarify your beliefs about this topic.

_____,

_____

_____

_____

_____

_____

_____

_____

_____

_____

_____

_____

_____

_____

_____

_____

_____,

_____

Confrontation!

2 Samuel 12:1–14

David's sinful deed was done. Scandalous whispers buzzed throughout the palace, but no one dared say a word to the king. His pregnant bride was a mute reminder of that fateful spring night when adultery stained the king's record. Not only adultery but murder . . . and hypocrisy . . . and deception . . . and a hushed cover-up.

While David kept his sin secret, his conscience kept him bound in a straitjacket of guilt. It wasn't until Nathan confronted him that he repented, open and broken before God.

I. Twelve Months in Retrospect

Before we look at Nathan's confrontation, let's review David's sin and the crushing effects it had on his life.

A. Adultery, murder, and hypocrisy. The adulterous act, the murderous scheme, the hypocritical words—David committed them all behind the closed door of secrecy. Not only were they done secretly, they were done willfully. The whole tangled web of sin was woven by David's own hand. Yet, while David kept his sin hidden from the eyes of others, God saw it all.

> But the thing that David had done was evil in the sight of the Lord. (2 Sam. 11:27b)

B. Guilt, illness, and silence. Notice how David describes his season of unrepentance.

> When I kept silent about my sin, my body wasted away
> Through my groaning all day long.
> For day and night Thy hand was heavy upon me;
> My vitality was drained away as with the fever heat of summer. (Ps. 32:3–4)

Dealing with Guilt

One psychologist describes guilt as the red light on our internal dashboard. When you see the light's feverish glare, you have a choice to make. You can either pull over, get out of the car, open the hood and see what's wrong; or you can smash the light with a hammer and keep driving.

The first option leads to fixing the problem; it makes you aware of the broken water hose or the cracked radiator or the low oil level. The second only relieves the symptoms. You may be able to keep the light from glaring, but after a few more miles, the whole engine might burn up.

> How do you treat guilt's red light? Do you take it seriously, stopping to analyze why it's flashing? Or do you smash it with the hammer you conveniently keep in the glove compartment of your conscience—and let your spiritual motor burn up?[1]

II. One Moment of Truth

In 2 Samuel 12, God stirs David's heart toward repentance through the bold confrontation of Nathan.

A. Sent by God. David had hidden his sins for too long. No doubt, there had been some raised eyebrows ... some putting two and two together ... but nobody had dared confront the king. Now it was time for him to face both the truth and the consequences of his wrong. So God sent Nathan to stand before the most powerful man in the nation and tell him to his face what he had denied for a year (v. 1a).

An Observation

Notice that God didn't send Nathan to confront David immediately after he committed adultery—or even after the murder. He doesn't always settle up with us in the springtime of our sin. Often, He waits until we've experienced a barren winter in our souls.

B. Encounter with the king. Wisely, Nathan approaches David indirectly; he holds up a mirror to David's heart in the form of a parable.

1. **Nathan's parable.**

> "There were two men in one city, the one rich and
> the other poor.
> The rich man had a great many flocks and herds.
> But the poor man had nothing except one little
> ewe lamb
> Which he bought and nourished;
> And it grew up together with him and his children.

---

1. If your red guilt light signals at the slightest hint that you may have done something wrong, you need to evaluate the source of your guilt. There are two kinds of guilt: true guilt, which comes from willfully disobeying God, and false guilt, which is brought on by the judgments and suggestions of man. For a further explanation of how you can determine the difference between the two, see *Guilt and Grace,* by Paul Tournier (San Francisco, Calif.: Harper and Row, Publishers, 1983).

It would eat of his bread and drink of his cup
and lie in his bosom,
And was like a daughter to him.
Now a traveler came to the rich man,
And he was unwilling to take from his own flock
or his own herd,
To prepare for the wayfarer who had come to
him;
Rather he took the poor man's ewe lamb and
prepared it for the man who had come to
him." (vv. 1b–4)

2. **David's reaction.** Quick and powerful, David's response
was like lightning tearing through a clear black night.

Then David's anger burned greatly against the
man, and he said to Nathan, "As the Lord lives,
surely the man who has done this deserves to
die. And he must make restitution for the lamb
fourfold, because he did this thing and had no
compassion." (vv. 5–6)

In that vulnerable moment, David was trapped by his own
reaction.

3. **God's message.** Then Nathan thrusts through David's heart
the sharp-edged words of truth.

"You are the man!" (v. 7a)

He goes on to name David's crimes and their punishment,
as told to him from the mouth of God.

"Thus says the Lord God of Israel, 'It is I who
anointed you king over Israel and it is I who
delivered you from the hand of Saul. I also gave
you your master's house and your master's wives
into your care, and I gave you the house of Israel
and Judah; and if that had been too little, I would
have added to you many more things like these!
Why have you despised the word of the Lord by
doing evil in His sight? You have struck down
Uriah the Hittite with the sword, have taken his
wife to be your wife, and have killed him with
the sword of the sons of Ammon. Now therefore,
the sword shall never depart from your house,
because you have despised Me and have taken
the wife of Uriah the Hittite to be your wife.' Thus
says the Lord, 'Behold, I will raise up evil against
you from your own household; I will even take
your wives before your eyes, and give them to

your companion, and he shall lie with your wives in broad daylight. Indeed you did it secretly, but I will do this thing before all Israel, and under the sun.' " (vv. 7b–12)

"Stripes that Wound . . ."

Nathan's confrontation must have hurt David. Yet it was this pain that stirred him to repentance and restored him to fellowship with his Lord.

If God has led you to confront someone in sin and you're hesitant to follow through, remember Solomon's counsel:

Stripes that wound scour away evil.

And strokes reach the innermost parts.

(Prov. 20:30; see also 27:6)

C. Repentance and restoration. Broken over his sin, David confesses it to Nathan.

Then David said to Nathan, "I have sinned against the Lord." (v. 13a)

Nathan's response salves David's guilt with God's grace.

And Nathan said to David, "The Lord also has taken away your sin; you shall not die." (v. 13b)

However, Nathan told David that God would take the life of his illegitimate son so that the Lord's enemies would have no reason to blaspheme God (v. 14).

III. Advice to Apply

Through the confrontation of Nathan, David's broken relationship with God was made whole. Let's take a moment to study the specifics of confrontation and repentance so that we can keep sin from shattering the spirits of others and ourselves.

A. Confrontation. For confrontation to be effective, it must be based on truth. It must also be done at the right time, not rushed or initiated from pure emotion. Also, the words used should be wise (see Prov. 25:11, 15:23). Finally, confrontation takes courage—it takes the risk of losing a friend or straining a relationship.

B. Repentance. True repentance includes open, unguarded admission, a desire to turn from the sin, a broken and humble spirit, and an acknowledgment of God's forgiveness and acceptance.

> ## "A Contrite Heart"
>
> After his confrontation with Nathan, David penned per-
> haps one of his most moving psalms—a psalm laced with
> an attitude of genuine repentance. Listen to his words.
> Hear the cry of his broken spirit. And you will know the
> heart of a man truly sorry for his sin.
>
> > Create in me a clean heart, O God,
> > And renew a steadfast spirit within me.
> > Do not cast me away from Thy presence,
> > And do not take Thy Holy Spirit from me.
> > Restore to me the joy of Thy salvation,
> > And sustain me with a willing spirit. . . .
> > O Lord, open my lips,
> > That my mouth may declare Thy praise.
> > For Thou dost not delight in sacrifice, otherwise
> >   I would give it;
> > Thou art not pleased with burnt offering.
> > The sacrifices of God are a broken spirit;
> > A broken and a contrite heart, O God, Thou wilt
> >   not despise. (Ps. 51:10–12, 15–17)
>
> If you find yourself bound by guilt today, confess your
> sin to the Father. If you come to Him with a broken and
> contrite heart, He will not condemn you.

 Living Insights

Study One

David enjoyed the passing pleasures of sin. However, what followed
was far from pleasant. David's thoughts from this time are recorded in
Psalms 32 and 51. Let's take some time to examine these two writings.

- In Psalm 32 we see the joy of being forgiven. However, it is preceded
  by a time of judgment. As you study this song, circle the words that
  stand out in your mind. Take special note of verse 8, where God begins to teach us. Jot down the lessons you learn from His instruction.

1. _____

_____

2. _____

_____

Continued on next page

113

3. _____

_____

4. _____

_____

- As you read Psalm 51, circle the key words. Feel the intense emotion
  flowing from David's pen. Write down the conclusions you reach that
  describe David, his sin, God, and His dealing with David.

  1. _____

  _____

  2. _____

  _____

  3. _____

  _____

  4. _____

  _____

 Living Insights

Study Two ▬▬▬▬▬▬▬▬▬▬▬▬▬▬▬▬▬▬▬▬▬▬▬▬

This lesson ended with two areas for application: confrontation and
repentance. Perhaps God has spoken to you about one of these issues.

- Does God want you to confront a friend who is not walking with
  Him? Review the four elements of successful confrontation.

Absolute truth	Wise wording
Right timing	Selfless courage

How does your approach measure up to this list? Which area is the
weakest for you? How can you strengthen it? Remember, confrontation is a serious matter, not to be taken lightly or to be entered into
hastily.

- Do you need to repent? Does your sin need to be confessed? In order to reach its full extent, repentance must include these four qualities:

> Open, unguarded admission
> Desire to make a complete break from the sin
> A humble, broken spirit
> Claiming God's forgiveness and acceptance

Are you in need of cleansing? Will you take God seriously and deal with this now? Spend some time thinking, reflecting, and talking with God.

Trouble at Home

2 Samuel 12–18, Galatians 6:7–8a

When a storm is raging, the best place to be is home, protected from the howling wind and the cold, rainy blasts.

That is, unless the blizzard is inside the home. Often, while the fireplace crackles warm and cozy sounds, the hearts within a home are chilled by the cold winds of compromise and tempestuous rebellion.

These storms can devastate a family like no amount of rain or snow ever could. And nobody who ignores God's Word is protected from them. As Hosea said:

> For they sow the wind,
> And they reap the whirlwind. (8:7a)

In spite of the fact that he was king, David was no exception to Hosea's principle. He had sown the wind with Bathsheba, and now he must reap the whirlwind.

I. Principle from Scripture

Galatians 6:7–8a lays it out plain and clear:

> Do not be deceived, God is not mocked; for whatever a man sows, this he will also reap. For the one who sows to his own flesh shall from the flesh reap corruption.

Notice that this passage doesn't offer an "unless" clause; it exempts no one—not even those with repentant hearts. The principle indelibly carved into the stone of these verses is that *we reap what we sow, forgiveness notwithstanding.* If you were to break an arm fighting, even if you restored your relationship with the other person, you would still be left with a broken arm. Likewise, when we sow sin, even after our communion with God has been restored, we must live with the consequences—we must endure the whirlwind.

II. Problems in the Palace

As we saw in the last lesson, Nathan not only confronted David's sin, he named the painful consequences that the king would endure.

A. General prediction. In just one simple but scathing weather report, Nathan predicted the storms in David's future.

> " 'Now therefore, the sword shall never depart from your house.' ... Thus says the Lord, 'Behold, I will raise up evil against you from your own household.' " (2 Sam. 12:10a, 11a)

B. Specific results. A survey of the events in 2 Samuel 12–18 will show how David reaped exactly what he had sown.

1. **Marital infidelity.** The first cloud on David's horizon is marital infidelity. God warned that just as David had taken another man's wife, so another man—someone close to him—would take his wives and lay with them; not secretly, but in broad daylight before all Israel.

> " 'I will even take your wives before your eyes, and
> give them to your companion, and he shall lie
> with your wives in broad daylight. Indeed you
> did it secretly, but I will do this thing before all
> Israel, and under the sun.' " (12:11b–12)

In chapter 16, we find this prediction fulfilled . . . by David's own son.

> So they pitched a tent for Absalom on the roof,
> and Absalom went in to his father's concubines
> in the sight of all Israel. (v. 22)

Notice where Absalom pitches his shameful tent. On the palace roof—the very place where David had sown the wind of adultery.

2. **Bathsheba's baby dies.** Soon after David and Bathsheba's son is born, the Lord strikes him with a sickness that takes his life.

> Then the Lord struck the child that Uriah's widow
> bore to David, so that he was very sick. David
> therefore inquired of God for the child; and David
> fasted and went and lay all night on the ground.
> And the elders of his household stood beside
> him in order to raise him up from the ground,
> but he was unwilling and would not eat food
> with them. Then it happened on the seventh day
> that the child died. And the servants of David
> were afraid to tell him that the child was dead,
> for they said, "Behold, while the child was still
> alive, we spoke to him and he did not listen to
> our voice. How then can we tell him that the
> child is dead, since he might do himself harm!"
> But when David saw that his servants were whis-
> pering together, David perceived that the child
> was dead; so David said to his servants, "Is the
> child dead?" And they said, "He is dead."
> (12:15b–19)

The storm is building, and with it, David's grief.

3. **Brother disgraces sister.** Chapter 13 brings us the sordid incident in which David's son Amnon rapes his half sister Tamar.

> Now it was after this that Absalom the son of
> David had a beautiful sister whose name was
> Tamar, and Amnon the son of David loved her.
> (v. 1)

But it was the wrong kind of love. It wasn't affectionate,
brotherly love. It was physical and incestuous.

> And Amnon was so frustrated because of his
> sister Tamar that he made himself ill, for she was
> a virgin, and it seemed hard to Amnon to do
> anything to her. (v. 2)

Taking the counsel of Jonadab, a wicked friend, Amnon
feigned sickness to get Tamar to care for him in his bed.
When she brought him something to eat,

> he took hold of her and said to her, "Come, lie
> with me, my sister." But she answered him, "No,
> my brother, do not violate me, for such a thing
> is not done in Israel; do not do this disgraceful
> thing!" (vv. 11b–12)

Refusing to listen to Tamar, he violates her. And his "love"
for her immediately sours to hatred (vv. 14–15).

4. Brother hates brother. When Absalom, Tamar's full brother,
finds out about the rape, the domestic storm becomes more
volatile.

> But Absalom did not speak to Amnon either good
> or bad; for Absalom hated Amnon because he
> had violated his sister Tamar. (v. 22)

Where was David when Amnon raped his half sister . . . where
was he when Absalom's hate raged against his brother?
"Now when King David heard of all these matters, he was
very angry," verse 21 states. But sadly, David's anger went
no further. Merrill Unger comments on David's pathetic in-
action throughout these turbulent events.

> Throughout all of this David showed his weak-
> ness and leniency because of his own failures
> and his giving in to the lusts of the flesh. *He was
> very angry,* and the Greek [Septuagint] adds, "But
> he vexed not the spirit of Amnon, his son, be-
> cause he loved him, because he was his first-
> born."[1]

5. Absalom murders Amnon. Absalom has waited two years
for David to act. But because of his father's passivity, Absalom's hatred festers into a plot to murder Amnon.

1. Merrill F. Unger, *Unger's Commentary on the Old Testament* (Chicago, Ill.: Moody Press,
1981), vol. 1, p. 430.

And Absalom commanded his servants, saying,
"See now, when Amnon's heart is merry with
wine, and when I say to you, 'Strike Amnon,' then
put him to death." . . . And the servants of Absalom
did to Amnon just as Absalom had commanded.
(vv. 28a, 29a)

6. **Absalom rebels and runs from home.** After David hears
about Amnon's death, Absalom flees to the home of his
grandfather—Talmai, king of Geshur. There, he nurses his
grudge and develops a scheme of rebellion against his father.

7. **Absalom leads a conspiracy.** The storm of David's life
continues to stir fiercely, as we find Absalom's heart filled
with revolt against his father. When a messenger tells David
of his son's conspiracy, David becomes afraid:

"Arise and let us flee, for otherwise none of us
shall escape from Absalom. Go in haste, lest he
overtake us quickly and bring down calamity on
us and strike the city with the edge of the sword."
(15:14b)

8. **Joab murders Absalom.** The storm comes to its tragic
end with the death of Absalom. As he is riding his mule,
Absalom passes under a great oak and catches his hair in
its thick branches. But the mule bolts, leaving him hanging.
And Joab, one of David's men, takes advantage of Absalom's
vulnerable position.

So he took three spears in his hand and thrust
them through the heart of Absalom while he was
yet alive in the midst of the oak. (18:14b)

When David got word of his son's death, he grieved deeply.

And the king was deeply moved and went up to
the chamber over the gate and wept. And thus
he said as he walked, "O my son Absalom, my
son, my son Absalom! Would I had died instead
of you, O Absalom, my son, my son!" (v. 33)

Was the passing pleasure of David's sin worth the devasta-
tion he reaped?

> ### *"God Is Not Mocked"*
> If you have taken lightly the grace of God . . . if you
> have childishly skipped through the corridors of the
> kingdom, picking and choosing sin or righteousness at
> will—you may be in for a domestic whirlwind. It might
> be that you're already reaping the consequences, or
> maybe the storm is just brewing on the horizon.

Though God's forgiveness is sure, so are sin's consequences. If you've begun to sow the wind of carnality, thinking that grace will cover it all, stop—before the weather of your life becomes difficult to endure.

Don't be deceived.

God's grace doesn't necessarily chase away the dark clouds of sin's consequences.

 Living Insights

Study One

David's family is just one of the tragic examples of the truth of Galatians 6:7–8a at work. Let's study a few more illustrations from the Scriptures.

- Look up the following passages and name the people who were involved, what sin was sown, and how they reaped the whirlwind of God's judgment. Notice the ironic relationship between each consequence and the sin it reflects.

Genesis 6:1–8, 7:17–24

_____

_____

_____

_____

_____

Judges 16:1–21

_____

_____

_____

_____

_____

Isaiah 14:12–17, Revelation 20:7–10

_____

_____

_____

_____

_____

_____

Acts 5:1–11

_____

_____

_____

_____

_____

🌺 *Living Insights*

Study Two ▬▬▬▬▬▬▬▬▬▬▬▬▬▬▬

People often misuse grace to justify their sin, never really considering the consequences. Yet Galatians 6:7–8a remains unalterable.

- *We reap what we sow, forgiveness notwithstanding.* Have you experienced this? Relate a few lessons from your past.

Sowing	Reaping

Continued on next page

Sowing	Reaping

- What about the present? Have you been sowing to your flesh? Are you beginning to reap the consequences? Write down some ideas on how to stop sowing sin.

Action plan: _____

_____

_____

_____

_____

_____

_____

_____

_____

_____

Riding Out the Storm

2 Samuel 12:13–25

It's midnight, Rockport, Maine. The harbor is quiet, except for the boats' creaking decks and the water slapping up against the wooden hulls.

But within minutes, storm clouds begin to tumble through the sky. Thunder rumbles, rain pelts. The tranquil little harbor is tossed by a whirlwind.

One boat, tied loosely to its moorings, snaps its rope and is carried out by the violent currents to crash upon the rocks.

But another boat—secured to the dock and firmly anchored—rides out the storm and is ready to sail when the sun comes out in the morning.

Our last lesson showed David in the center of the whirlwind, reaping the results of his sin. In today's study, we'll see how he weathered the storm—whether he sank or survived—and why. We'll see that when the waves of sin's consequences begin to slosh the decks of our lives, our only hope for survival is to anchor ourselves to the Lord.

I. A Principle in Review

Before learning about how to ride out a storm, let's review the principle that predicts the gusty weather sin often brings our way.

A. Stated in words. The principle is twofold. First, *we reap what we sow, forgiveness notwithstanding.* Forgiveness doesn't necessarily erase the consequences of our sin. And second, *the pain of the reaping eclipses the pleasure of the sowing.* The suffering you'll endure in the whirlwind is much greater than the pleasure of sowing the wind.

B. Supported in Scripture. Support for the two strands of this principle is found throughout Scripture.

1. **Hosea 8:7a.**
   For they sow the wind,
   And they reap the whirlwind.

2. **Romans 6:21.**
   What benefit were you then deriving from the things of which you are now ashamed? For the outcome of those things is death.

3. **Galatians 6:7–8a.**
   Do not be deceived, God is not mocked; for whatever a man sows, this he will also reap. For the one who sows to his own flesh shall from the flesh reap corruption.

4. **Proverbs 6:27–29.**
   Can a man take fire in his bosom,
   And his clothes not be burned?

Or can a man walk on hot coals,
And his feet not be scorched?
So is the one who goes in to his neighbor's wife;
Whoever touches her will not go unpunished.

II. David's Experience and Example

David and his family reaped the whirlwind of his sin with Bathsheba. Yet, when the waves of domestic tragedy threatened to sink his life, he humbly anchored his faith to the Lord.

A. Acknowledgment of the sowing. David responded to Nathan's confrontation with an honest confession.

> Then David said to Nathan, "I have sinned against the Lord." And Nathan said to David, "The Lord also has taken away your sin; you shall not die." (2 Sam. 12:13)

Notice that because David acknowledged his sin, God spared his life (v. 13b). Under the Law, adulterers were to be stoned. But because of His grace, God chose to send consequences that were less severe than what David deserved.

B. Response during the reaping. Nathan told David that the first gust of the whirlwind would be the death of his infant son (v. 14). And with that prediction, David had to decide how to react. Like the boat that was loosed from its moorings, his life could have ended up broken on the rocks of bitterness. But instead, he dropped four anchors of faith that helped him ride out the storm.

   1. He prayed. David was faced with the first consequence of his sin soon after it was predicted.

> Then the Lord struck the child that Uriah's widow bore to David, so that he was very sick. David therefore inquired of God for the child; and David fasted and went and lay all night on the ground. And the elders of his household stood beside him in order to raise him up from the ground, but he was unwilling and would not eat food with them. (vv. 15b–17)

A Time to Be Silent

While enduring this deep pain, David stayed home where he could be quiet and alone with God.

If, like David, you're enduring sin's storm, take time to be quiet. In this soul-searching period of your life, spend time alone with God, listen to His voice, and let Him minister to your heart.

---

2. **He faced the consequences realistically.** After seven days, the infant died. David's servants were afraid to tell him, concerned that, in the depths of his sorrow, he might take his own life (v. 18). But look at David's mature response to the painful news.

> But when David saw that his servants were whispering together, David perceived that the child was dead; so David said to his servants, "Is the child dead?" And they said, "He is dead." So David arose from the ground, washed, anointed himself, and changed his clothes; and he came into the house of the Lord and worshiped.[1] (vv. 19–20a)

David accepted this painful consequence, refusing to blame God or become bitter.

Bitterness or Humility?

Bitterness can cause your faith to fray and snap, sending you out into the violent sea to weather the storm alone. But a humble heart will accept the storm and anchor itself to God's love.

How do you respond in the whirlwind? As sin's consequences wash over your life, do you shake your fist at God—or lift your hands in prayer?

---

3. **He claimed God's truths.** In verses 20b–23, we see that David's heart was secured in belief.

> Then he came to his own house, and when he requested, they set food before him and he ate. Then his servants said to him, "What is this thing that you have done? While the child was alive, you fasted and wept; but when the child died, you arose and ate food." And he said, "While the child was still alive, I fasted and wept; for I said, 'Who knows, the Lord may be gracious to me, that the child may live.' But now he has died; why should I fast? Can I bring him back again? I shall go to him, but he will not return to me."

David's response shows that he believed in the hope of heaven. He knew his son was gone, but he also knew that

---

1. David's spirit of worship is much like Job's after he suffered the loss of his children (see Job 1:21–22).

one day he would see him again. Even in the midst of his suffering, David relied on God's truth. What about you? When you experience the consequences of sin, do you turn to God's Word for comfort?

4. **He went on, refusing to give up.** After the funeral ... after mourning his loss, David found the grace to live again.

> Then David comforted his wife Bathsheba, and went in to her and lay with her; and she gave birth to a son, and he named him Solomon. Now the Lord loved him. (v. 24)

Grace to Go On

It takes God's grace not only to endure the whirlwind but also to move on once the storm has calmed.

If you've experienced the results of sin in your life and are still slumped in the corner licking your wounds, it's time to pick yourself up and move on. God has forgiven you, but you must accept His grace and forgive yourself.

Soon after David's loss, he held a new baby son in his arms. Likewise, neither will God punish you forever; He is not through blessing your life.

III. Observations to Be Made

Along with the guidelines we've studied, several general observations can be made about riding out the storm.

A. It's a lonely experience. You will never be more alone than when you are in the whirlwind of sin's consequences. Others may want to help, but you alone will experience the depth of your pain.

B. It's a learning experience. It's a time to stay sensitive to God's voice.

C. It's a temporary experience. You may feel like it will last forever, but it won't. It will end. He will see you through.

D. It's a humbling experience. Look at what Moses wanted the Israelites to remember from their wilderness wanderings:

> "And you shall remember all the way which the Lord your God has led you in the wilderness these forty years, that He might humble you, testing you, to know what was in your heart.... And He humbled you and let you be hungry." (Deut. 8:2a, 3a)

When you're going through the whirlwind, you won't be experiencing fruitfulness in your life. It will be a harsh time, a barren time. To humble you, God will let you be hungry for His blessings—that's how much He values a contrite heart. God takes sin seriously. Won't you take it just as seriously?

 Living Insights

Study One ▬▬▬▬▬▬▬▬▬▬▬▬▬▬▬▬▬▬▬▬▬▬▬▬▬▬▬▬▬▬

The pain of the reaping eclipses the pleasure of the sowing. Tucked away in the prophetic section of the Old Testament is a book that deals with that very subject. The book is Lamentations, written by the prophet Jeremiah. Only five chapters long, it is a sobering scenario of reaping the whirlwind.

- This would be an appropriate time to unhurriedly consider this book. As you read it, write down insights that come to your mind, especially involving the consequences of sin.

References	Consequences of Sin

Continued on next page

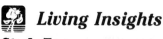 *Living Insights*

We've learned several lessons about dealing with sin's consequences. Let's spend a few minutes making them personal.

- Are you currently experiencing the consequences of sin? If so, how would you describe your experience? Put a check by the most appropriate phrase.

  ☐ A problem

  ☐ A predicament

  ☐ A crisis

  ☐ A panic

  ☐ A shock

- How are you responding to the whirlwind? We've studied four aspects of a proper response. Which is the easiest for you? Put a check by it. Which is the toughest? Circle it. Write out some reasons why these are easy or tough.

  1. Pray   3. Claim God's truths

  2. Face consequences realistically   4. Refuse to give up

Reasons: _____

_____

_____

_____

_____

_____

_____

_____

_____

- Are you lonely? Learning? Feeling like it will never end? Humbled? Which of these best describes your situation? It's time to settle up with God. Face Him realistically. Verbalize your thoughts to Him in prayer.

Friends in Need

2 Samuel 15–19

Samuel Taylor Coleridge was a melancholy genius. Born in Devonshire, England, the youngest of thirteen, his brilliance shone at an early age. And today, critics agree that his literary contributions are considerable.

His life, however, did not fare so well. Before he was thirty, he was victimized by rheumatism. He tried to temper his pain with opium, and, as a result, he became addicted—and lonely. But he found a friend in William Wordsworth, whom he was closer to than his wife. Unfortunately, though, he fell in love with Wordsworth's sister-in-law, and his already shaky marriage crumbled. In time his opium addiction became worse, alienating even Wordsworth, and leaving Coleridge at the lowest point of his life. Eventually, though, he was able to control his habit, and he and Wordsworth renewed their rich friendship.

His most famous work is probably the epic poem *The Rime of the Ancient Mariner.* Although rarely recognized, among his best works is *Youth and Age,* a collection of his observations about life. In this reflective work, we see that through all the pain and loneliness he endured, he found a shelter in his relationship with Wordsworth. He wrote:

> Friendship is a sheltering tree.[1]

Like Coleridge, we all need friends—those great, green trees that spread their leafy limbs over us and shelter us from the hot rays of adversity or from winter's lonely wind. And David was no exception. In this lesson, we will see him in desperate need of shelter, and we'll learn some essential things about friendship from those who stood faithfully by his side.

I. The Truth about Friends

Scripture underscores the importance of friendship by making more than one hundred references to it. Before examining its value in David's life, let's take a look at some truths about friends in general.

A. Friends are essential, not optional. There is no substitute for a friend—someone to care, to listen, to comfort, even to reprove (see Prov. 27:6, 17).

B. Friends must be cultivated; they're not automatic. "Friendship is to be purchased only by friendship. A man may have authority over others, but he can never have their heart but by giving his own."[2]

1. Samuel Taylor Coleridge, in *Bartlett's Familiar Quotations,* 15th ed., rev. and enl., ed. Emily Morison Beck (Boston, Mass.: Little, Brown and Co., 1980), p. 436.

2. Thomas Wilson, in *Speaker's Encyclopedia of Stories Quotations and Anecdotes,* by Jacob M. Braude (Englewood Cliffs, N.J.: Prentice-Hall, 1955), p. 155.

C. Friends impact our lives; they're not neutral. Those we are close to rub off on us, change us. Their morals and philosophies, convictions and character eventually become our own (see 1 Cor. 15:33, Ps. 1:1, Prov. 13:20).

D. Friends come in four classifications, not one. As we look at the different levels of friendship, notice how the number of friends we have in each of the categories *decreases* the further down the list we go. But honesty *increases* in these friendships.

1. **Acquaintances.** Acquaintances are those with whom you have infrequent contact and shallow interaction. They don't ask deep questions, but skate through the relationship on the ice of superficiality.
2. **Casual friends.** With these people you have more contact, common interests, and you feel comfortable asking more specific questions.
3. **Close friends.** With close friends you share life goals, the freedom to ask personal questions, and meaningful projects.
4. **Intimate friends.** With intimate friends, you have regular contact and a deep commitment to mutual character development. You share the freedom to criticize and correct, encourage and embrace. They are your sheltering trees.

II. The Needs in David's Life

Because of his tragic season of compromise, David needed shelter and support in three areas of his life.

A. Personally. David was almost destroyed by guilt. He had committed adultery with Bathsheba, killed Uriah, and lived a life of lies. He had brought shame to God's name, and his world began to crumble.

B. Domestically. David's home was shattered by a domestic whirlwind: his baby son died; another son raped a sister; and another son, Absalom, killed his brother and led a rebellious conspiracy against David's throne.

C. Politically. Driven from the throne by Absalom, David's political career was fractured.

III. The Crisis to Withstand

Absalom cleverly maneuvered himself into a place of political strength by winning the hearts of all Israel (2 Sam. 15:1–12). His conspiracy worked; David fled in fear of his life (vv. 13–18). The hot Palestinian sun of hardship beating down on his brow, David desperately needed friendship's sheltering tree.

IV. The People Who Stood Near

To meet David's needs, God sent him not just one friend but a group of faithful supports. Though their names are obscure, the nature of their friendship shines clearly to enlighten us all.

A. Ittai. Many accompanied David when he fled from Absalom, including Ittai, a man from Gath whom David had brought into exile when he stormed Philistia after defeating Goliath (vv. 19–20). But David encouraged Ittai to return home for his safety. Listen to Ittai's reply:

> But Ittai answered the king and said, "As the Lord lives, and as my lord the king lives, surely wherever my lord the king may be, whether for death or for life, there also your servant will be." (v. 21)

So Ittai and his men—once David's enemies—became his loyal supporters (v. 22).

Friendship: Thicker Than Blood

When everyone else has turned away, there will be a few who will say, "I'm with you. Count on me. I'm here."

One might even be a person from Gath—a person who had been your enemy, but who has come full circle to become your friend.

Blood ties don't always guarantee friendship. David's son became an enemy, while the king's enemies—those of other blood lines—proved to be his friends.

Is the friendship you offer others thicker than blood?

B. Zadok and Abiathar. These priests wanted to support David, bringing the ark of the covenant with them (v. 24). But, feeling that their godly influence might soften Absalom's heart, David asked that they remain in Jerusalem. Even though returning to Absalom might bring them hardship, loss, suffering, and possibly death, they were willing to do as David requested, with no argument (v. 29).

A Sheltering Tree

Are you a Zadok or an Abiathar in another's life? Are you willing to endure the unrelenting rays of hardship's sun to help a friend who needs you?

C. Hushai. Hushai came to David wearing signs of compassion—a torn robe and dust on his head (v. 32). He was ready to stay by David's side. But David had another plan in mind for Hushai: espionage.

> And David said to him, "If you pass over with me, then you will be a burden to me. But if you return to the city, and say to Absalom, 'I will be your servant,

O king; as I have been your father's servant in time past, so I will now be your servant,' then you can thwart the counsel of Ahithophel[3] for me. . . . So it shall be that whatever you hear from the king's house, you shall report to Zadok and Abiathar the priests. Behold their two sons are with them there, Ahimaaz, Zadok's son and Jonathan, Abiathar's son; and by them you shall send me everything that you hear." (vv. 33–36)

Without questioning, and without being offended that David chose not to take him along, Hushai obeyed.

So Hushai, David's friend, came into the city, and Absalom came into Jerusalem. (v. 37)

D. Shobi, Machir, and Barzillai. Realizing that David and his men were tired and hungry in the wilderness, these three friends met their physical needs.

Now when David had come to Mahanaim, Shobi the son of Nahash from Rabbah of the sons of Ammon, Machir the son of Ammiel from Lo-debar, and Barzillai the Gileadite from Rogelim, brought beds, basins, pottery, wheat, barley, flour, parched grain, beans, lentils, parched seeds, honey, curds, sheep, and cheese of the herd, for David and for the people who were with him, to eat; for they said, "The people are hungry and weary and thirsty in the wilderness." (17:27–29)

Without being asked, these three came to David's aid. They brought not just the basics but went all out with a gourmet meal.[4]

E. Joab. When Absalom died, David hit bottom (18:33). Trapped in a cave of grief, he needed a friend to climb in and pull him out. The friend God sent was Joab.

And the king covered his face and cried out with a loud voice, "O my son Absalom, O Absalom, my son, my son!" Then Joab came into the house to the king and said, "Today you have covered with shame the faces of all your servants, who today have saved your life and the lives of your sons and daughters, the

---

3. Ahithophel, once David's sagacious counselor, defected to Absalom when he revolted against his father's throne. Interestingly, his name means "brother of foolishness."

4. Each of these men had good reason *not* to help David, yet they gave sacrificially and without being asked. Shobi's people—the Ammonites—were David's enemies. Machir from Lo-debar was the one who had taken in Jonathan's son Mephibosheth (2 Sam. 9:4–5)—he had done his share of favors for David. And Barzillai was old; he could have considered himself retired and sent someone younger.

lives of your wives, and the lives of your concubines, by loving those who hate you, and by hating those who love you. For you have shown today that princes and servants are nothing to you; for I know this day that if Absalom were alive and all of us were dead today, then you would be pleased. Now therefore arise, go out and speak kindly to your servants, for I swear by the Lord, if you do not go out, surely not a man will pass the night with you, and this will be worse for you than all the evil that has come upon you from your youth until now." (19:4–7)

Joab dared to confront David. The king's tears were drowning his sensitivity to his people—men and women who had risked their lives to save him. And they were demoralized (v. 3). David's leadership was needed; it was time for him to get back on the throne.

A Closing Thought

Sheltering trees.

Coleridge had Wordsworth, whose friendship helped protect him from the cold blasts of his personal pain.

David had his group of friends to support him during his turbulent times.

Has God called you to be someone's sheltering tree? To bring the food, run the errands, jeopardize your personal comfort, even to confront? If so, give ... support ... cover your friend in the umbrella of your branches—provide security and rest.

 Living Insights

Study One

Our lesson surveyed five key chapters in 2 Samuel. In them, we saw that David had a need for friends. His family was in the midst of crumbling, and 2 Samuel 15–19 revealed some friends who stood by David as true companions. Yet this same passage has its sad moments as well, as we see the bitterness and rebellion welling up in David's son Absalom.

● Reread these five chapters, and jot down your observations regarding both David's and Absalom's personalities and characters during all the turmoil. Do you see similarities? Obvious differences?

Continued on next page

David	
References	Observations

Absalom	
References	Observations

 *Living Insights*

"A man, sir, should keep his friendship in a constant repair."[5] How's your friendship factor? Use the following comments to prod your thinking in this respect.

• What do you find most satisfying about your friendships?

• How would you like to improve your friendships?

• After each category, jot down the names that come to mind:

Acquaintances—

Casual friends—

Close friends—

Intimate friends—

• What do you need to work on in order to cultivate friendship?

• How have you been impacted by your friends? Close by talking to God about your friendship with Him.

5. Samuel Johnson, in *Bartlett's Familiar Quotations,* p. 354.

Being Big Enough to Forgive

2 Samuel 16:5–13, 19:16–23

A hungry tramp was looking for a handout in a quaint old village some time ago. He came upon an interesting inn, a pub that had the unique name, "The Inn of Saint George and the Dragon." He went in sheepishly. It was rather a nice place.

He rapped on the kitchen door, and soon a woman walked up. She was the cook, and she said to him, "What do you want?" He was tattered and obviously dirty from having lived in the streets. And he said, "Please, ma'am, could you spare a bite for me to eat?" And she responded, "A bite to eat for a no-good bum? No! Go get a job like anybody else and work for your food!"

He walked out and was about halfway down the street when he turned around and looked back at the sign swinging out in front. It read: "The Inn of Saint George and the Dragon." He went back and knocked on the door again and said, "Well, ma'am, if Saint George is in, may I speak to him this time?"[1]

Like the callous cook, we often make people ask a second time to get past the dragon inside of us. We'd rather sit on the judgment seat than the mercy seat.

It takes an awfully big person to forgive. As we'll see in this lesson, David was that big. Are you? By the time we finish today's study, you'll know.

I. Some Initial Thoughts on Forgiveness

When we've been hurt, we often play at forgiving instead of offering true forgiveness.

A. Common reactions.

1. **Conditional forgiveness.** Conditional forgivers tell their offenders, "I will forgive you if . . . as soon as . . . whenever . . ." Like fiery dragons, they wait for you to make your next move so they can determine whether they'll back off or blow you away.

2. **Partial forgiveness.** Those who forgive only part way say, "I'll forgive, but don't expect me to forget . . . but don't let it happen again . . . but just get out of my life."

3. **Delayed forgiveness.** People who offer this type of forgiveness say, "I'll forgive you. Just give me some time—don't push."

---

1. This story is a paraphrase; its source is unknown.

B. The downward plunge. When we refuse to forgive, our lives begin taking a staircase downward. If forgiveness isn't given at each step, the next step will be unavoidable, and we will soon find ourselves in the dank dungeon of bitter revenge.

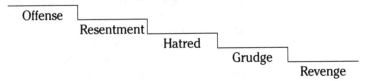

Offense
Resentment
Hatred
Grudge
Revenge

Making the Upward Climb

If you find yourself on this downward staircase, it's not too late to turn around and head back up toward the light. As Paul said:

> As those who have been chosen of God, holy and beloved, put on a heart of compassion, kindness, humility, gentleness and patience; bearing with one another, and forgiving each other, whoever has a complaint against anyone; *just as the Lord forgave you, so also should you.* (Col. 3:12–13, emphasis added; see also Eph. 4:32, Luke 6:37)

Remember the forgiveness God has lavished upon you. Give it freely to those who have hurt you. Then you will begin the upward climb toward spiritual freedom.[2]

II. An Example of Complete Forgiveness

A. A review of David's circumstances.
David's life had hit rock bottom. His affair with Bathsheba had set off a whole chain of tragic events: his infant son died, his family was in turmoil, he lost his throne to his rebellious son Absalom. Stripped of his dignity and political power, David had reached the lowest level of his life.

B. An account of Shimei's offense.
  1. **Shimei's harassment.** David was already down when, out of nowhere, there came a man, Shimei, to give him another kick.
     > When King David came to Bahurim, behold, there came out from there a man of the family of the house of Saul whose name was Shimei, the son

---

2. One of the most honest discussions on forgiveness is found in *Forgive and Forget: Healing the Hurts We Don't Deserve,* by Lewis B. Smedes (San Francisco, Calif.: Harper and Row, Publishers, 1984).

of Gera; he came out cursing continually as he came. And he threw stones at David and at all the servants of King David; and all the people and all the mighty men were at his right hand and at his left. And thus Shimei said when he cursed, "Get out, get out, you man of bloodshed, and worthless fellow! The Lord has returned upon you all the bloodshed of the house of Saul, in whose place you have reigned; and the Lord has given the kingdom into the hand of your son Absalom. And behold, you are taken in your own evil, for you are a man of bloodshed!" (16:5–8)

Shimei's accusations were nothing but false. David hadn't murdered members of Saul's household, neither had he stolen Saul's throne.

2. **Abishai's counsel.** In the face of these insulting charges, Zeruiah's son Abishai rose hotly to David's defense—and forgiveness was the farthest thing from his mind. He offered to avenge the offense with his own hands.

> Then Abishai the son of Zeruiah said to the king, "Why should this dead dog curse my lord the king? Let me go over now, and cut off his head." (v. 9)

3. **David's response.** But David chose not to take offense. His eyes were on God instead of Shimei, and he believed that it was all part of God's plan.

> But the king said, "What have I to do with you, O sons of Zeruiah? If he curses, and if the Lord has told him, 'Curse David,' then who shall say, 'Why have you done so?'" Then David said to Abishai and to all his servants, "Behold, my son who came out from me seeks my life; how much more now this Benjamite? Let him alone and let him curse, for the Lord has told him. Perhaps the Lord will look on my affliction and return good to me instead of his cursing this day." (vv. 10–12)

C. **Shimei's confession and David's response.** The story jumps from chapter 16 to chapter 19 where Absalom had just been killed. The revolt had ended, and David was brought back to the throne. A new spirit of optimism buoyed the Israelites' hearts. Suddenly, Shimei showed up, this time singing a different tune.

> So he said to the king, "Let not my lord consider me guilty, nor remember what your servant did wrong

on the day when my lord the king came out from Jerusalem, so that the king should take it to heart. For your servant knows that I have sinned; therefore behold, I have come today, the first of all the house of Joseph to go down to meet my lord the king." (19:19–20)

Shimei asked for forgiveness, and now the ball was in David's court. Again Abishai counseled David to kill Shimei (v. 21). However, this time David not only overlooked the offense but granted Shimei grace.

David then said, "What have I to do with you, O sons of Zeruiah, that you should this day be an adversary to me? Should any man be put to death in Israel today? For do I not know that I am king over Israel today?" And the king said to Shimei, "You shall not die." Thus the king swore to him. (vv. 22–23)

David was able to forgive Shimei for two reasons. First, his vertical focus was clear and strong—he had left the offense in God's hands (16:12). Second, he was aware of his own failure—he had come fresh off a humbling experience caused by his own sins.

The Fragrance of Forgiveness

"Forgiveness is the fragrance the violet sheds on the heel that has crushed it."[3]

III. Some Practical Suggestions

It's easy to talk about forgiveness, but it's hard to put it into practice. Below are several suggestions for tempering the dragon in us that wants to breathe fire when it's been burned.

A. **Develop a thicker layer of skin.** When you walk through thorns, you need to wear heavy boots. Likewise, when you walk in the path of people whose words nettle you, you've got to develop a thick skin. Ask God to substitute your china-doll feelings with tough-skinned resilience.

B. **Try to understand where your offender is coming from.** Look beyond the offense to the hurt little boy or girl within the person lashing out. Try to understand why that person might be taking a swing at you, and respond with grace.

C. **Recall times in your life when you have needed forgiveness.** This kind of thinking will build your tolerance for

---

3. *Speaker's Encyclopedia of Stories Quotations and Anecdotes,* by Jacob M. Braude (Englewood Cliffs, N.J.: Prentice-Hall, 1955), p. 150.

others and prompt you to forgive. The forgiven make the best forgivers.

D. Openly declare forgiveness and go on from there. The words "I forgive you" are the best therapy for both the offender and the offended. If you've been offended, free yourself and the one who has hurt you with a verbal gift of grace—and move on.

 Living Insights

Study One ▬▬▬▬▬▬▬▬▬▬▬▬▬▬▬▬▬▬▬▬▬▬▬▬▬▬▬▬▬▬▬▬

Have you ever studied what Scripture says about forgiveness? It's a vital topic that's worth our consideration.

- Let's focus on the New Testament. Below you will find a few of the key references which use the word *forgive* or *forgiveness*. Look up each verse and see if you can state its principle in one sentence.

Matthew 6:12 _____

_____

Mark 1:4 _____

_____

Luke 7:47 _____

_____

Acts 10:43 _____

_____

2 Corinthians 2:10 _____

_____

Ephesians 1:7 _____

_____

 Living Insights

Study Two ▬▬▬▬▬▬▬▬▬▬▬▬▬▬▬▬▬▬▬▬▬▬▬▬▬▬▬▬▬▬▬▬

After taking this look into David's life, it's possible that you've been reminded of someone you need to forgive. If that's true, answer the questions on the following page.

- Who is your Shimei? Who seems to take delight in kicking you when you're down?

  _____

- Have you resisted forgiving? Where are you in this downward plunge: offense . . . resentment . . . hatred . . . grudge . . . revenge?

  _____

- How does Proverbs 18:19 apply to your situation?

  _____

  _____

  _____

- Let's work on a strategy together.

  1. How can you develop a thicker layer of skin?

  _____

  _____

  2. Why does this person behave so offensively? Where do you think he or she might be coming from?

  _____

  _____

  3. Can you recall times when you have needed forgiveness? What was it like for you?

  _____

  _____

  4. What will it take for you to verbally declare your forgiveness?

  _____

  _____

  _____

A Song of Triumph

2 Samuel 22

As we continue our study of David, we begin to see the long shadows of age and pressure stretching across his life. Now in his twilight years, David has experienced several difficult events that have brought him to his knees before God: he lost his son Absalom (2 Sam. 18:32–33); a severe famine struck the land (21:1); and war with Philistia was rekindled (21:15).

Weary from his struggles, David found rest in God's faithful care and composed a triumphant song. In today's study, we will explore four themes from his hymn of praise to God, his deliverer.

I. First Theme: When Times Are Tough, the Lord Is Our Only Security (2 Samuel 22:2–20)

David describes what he felt during the stormy times as "violence" (v. 3), "waves of death" (v. 5), "torrents of destruction" (v. 5), "distress" (v. 7), "calamity" (v. 19). But he found a shelter in the Lord.

> "The Lord is my rock and my fortress and my deliverer;
> My God, my rock, in whom I take refuge;
> My shield and the horn of my salvation, my stronghold
>   and my refuge;
> My savior, Thou dost save me from violence. . . .
> He delivered me from my strong enemy,
> From those who hated me, for they were too strong for me.
> They confronted me in the day of my calamity,
> But the Lord was my support." (vv. 2–3, 18–19)

Though your enemies deal harshly with you, the Lord will tenderly support you in your despair. Why is He so faithful? What keeps His strong arms always open, always willing to hold you when you need Him? David gives the answer in a simple phrase profound with grace: "'He rescued me, because He delighted in me'" (v. 20b). Are times difficult in your life? Are you running from the enemy of loneliness—or pain? Like David, you can say, "He delights in me." Caring for you, He feels your ache. Delighting in you, He will be your support.

II. Second Theme: When Days Are Dark, the Lord Is Our Only Light (2 Samuel 22:21–31)

Even in his darkest times, David found a lamp to light his way:

> "For Thou art my lamp, O Lord;
> And the Lord illumines my darkness." (v. 29)

Carrying a lantern into a forest's night doesn't guarantee you'll see all the trees. It only means that you can see a few steps ahead of you, far enough to keep your footing sure. Likewise, as the Lord lights your path, He may not shine all the answers to the shadowy questions in your mind, but He will give you all the light you need to scale life's obstacles with confidence and agility.

> "For by Thee I can run upon a troop;
> By my God I can leap over a wall." (v. 30)

David also pictures the Lord as his lamp in Psalm 27:

> The Lord is my light and my salvation;
> Whom shall I fear?
> The Lord is the defense of my life;
> Whom shall I dread? (v. 1)

Is there fear in your life? Fear of failure ... fear of the unknown ... fear of financial disaster ... fear of losing someone you love? Remember, His light is yours ... His Word is sure. " 'He is a shield to all who take refuge in Him' " (2 Sam. 22:31b).

III. Third Theme: When Our Walk Is Weak, the Lord Is Our Only Strength (2 Samuel 22:32–49)

David was by no means a strong man in himself. In fact, when he was ruled by his own passions, his seemingly solid-marble character proved to be cracked and chipped and flawed. The key to David's strength was that He acknowledged God as its source.

> "God is my strong fortress;
> And He sets the blameless in His way.
> He makes my feet like hinds' feet,
> And sets me on my high places.
> He trains my hands for battle,
> So that my arms can bend a bow of bronze.
> Thou hast also given me the shield of Thy salvation,
> And Thy help makes me great." (vv. 33–36)

The apostle Paul, also pointing to the Lord as the source of his strength, writes a New Testament version of this theme:

> And because of the surpassing greatness of the revelations, for this reason, to keep me from exalting myself, there was given me a thorn in the flesh, a messenger of Satan to buffet me—to keep me from exalting myself! Concerning this I entreated the Lord three times that it might depart from me. And He has said to me, "My grace is sufficient for you, for power is perfected in weakness." Most gladly, therefore, I will rather boast about my weaknesses, that the power of Christ may dwell in me. Therefore I am well content with weaknesses, with insults, with distresses, with persecutions, with difficulties, for Christ's sake; *for when I am weak, then I am strong.* (2 Cor. 12:7–10, emphasis added)

IV. Fourth Theme: When Our Future Is Foggy, the Lord Is Our Only Hope (2 Samuel 22:50–51)

As David finished his song, he showed that his heart was soft, not bitter—that thanksgiving and praise were on his lips.

> "Therefore I will give thanks to Thee, O Lord, among the
> nations,
> And I will sing praises to Thy name." (v. 50)

He was filled with the hope of deliverance, protection, and loving-kindness—not only to him but to all his descendants as well.

> "He is a tower of deliverance to His king,
> And shows lovingkindness to His anointed,
> To David and his descendants forever." (v. 51)

Is your future foggy? Are you unsure of what tomorrow holds? Parts of your future will always be a mystery to you. But there are a few things you *can* count on as God's child—promises that cut through the clouds like shafts of sunlight:

> Through God we shall do valiantly,
> And it is He who will tread down our adversaries.
> (Ps. 60:12)

> The steps of a man are established by the Lord;
> And He delights in his way.
> When he falls, he shall not be hurled headlong;
> Because the Lord is the One who holds his hand.
> (Ps. 37:23–24)[1]

A Concluding Thought

We don't need to wait until the long shadows of age and pressure overtake us to stop and take a close, hard look at our lives. Are there tough times in your life? Have there been dark days? Is there a weakened walk? A foggy future? Only the Lord of security...light...strength...and hope can see you through. Won't you cling closely to Him during your struggles—and make David's song of triumph your own?

 Living Insights

Study One ▰▰▰▰▰▰▰▰▰▰▰▰▰▰▰▰▰▰▰▰▰▰▰▰▰▰▰

David's psalm in 2 Samuel 22 is rich in theme. However, its themes aren't solely its own; they're shared by many of the other psalms David

---

1. Scripture is full of hope and promise for our futures. For a complete list of God's promises, see *The Bible Promise Book* (Westwood, N.J.: Barbour and Co., 1985).

wrote during the trying days of his life. Let's take some time to uncover the four themes of this psalm in some of David's other songs of praise to the Lord.

- Under each theme, look up the references given and paraphrase the truth you find. Let this exercise reinforce what you've learned through this lesson—that our God is a God of security, light, strength, and hope.

1. *When times are tough, the Lord is our only security.*

Psalm 9:9 _____

_____

Psalm 31:20 _____

_____

Psalm 32:7 _____

_____

2. *When days are dark, the Lord is our only light.*

Psalm 18:28 _____

_____

Psalm 27:1a _____

_____

3. *When our walk is weak, the Lord is our only strength.*

Psalm 31:4 _____

_____

Psalm 144:1–2 _____

_____

_____

_____

Continued on next page

4. *When our future is foggy, the Lord is our only hope.*

Psalm 71:5 _____

_____

Psalm 104:27–28 _____

_____

_____

_____

📖 *Living Insights*

Study Two ▬▬▬▬▬▬▬▬▬

Long before David was a king, he was a composer. His feelings came through clearly in his songs.

- Have you ever written a song or poem to God? Why not use this Living Insights time to give it a try? Don't worry about rhythm and rhyme, just let your praise to God flow from your pen. Perhaps you'd like to expand on one of the four themes David developed in 2 Samuel 22. Whatever you choose to do, use this as a time to try something different in offering praise and worship to God.

_____

_____

_____

_____

_____

_____

_____

_____

_____

_____

_____

_____

When the Godly Are Foolish

2 Samuel 24, 1 Chronicles 21

Most children outgrow their foolish ways. As they mature, they shed the name-calling, the my-dad-is-bigger-than-your-dad mentality, the steady diet of candy and gum.

But sadly, even as God's children, we never outgrow our worst habit: sin. We are never immune from its appeal. In fact, those who fall the hardest are often those who have walked the longest with God. And when spiritual leaders fall, they usually take a host of innocent people with them.

In today's study, we see David—gray at his ruddy temples—make a foolish decision based on pride. The consequences of his choice are staggering, and they remind us all of the seriousness of our sin.

I. Analysis of the Decision

In the latter years of David's reign, probably on the heels of a Philistine-Israeli war, a series of skirmishes had taken place in which David and his soldiers had killed more giants from Gath (1 Chron. 20). Again, fresh from victory, David was vulnerable.

A. Generally. Wanting to reinforce his sense of military security and pride, David commanded Joab to take a census.

> And the king said to Joab the commander of the army who was with him, "Go about now through all the tribes of Israel, from Dan to Beersheba, and register the people, that I may know the number of the people." (2 Sam. 24:2)

Joab was aware of his sinful motives and questioned him openly.

> But Joab said to the king, "Now may the Lord your God add to the people a hundred times as many as they are, while the eyes of my lord the king still see; but why does my lord the king delight in this thing?" (v. 3)

But David arrogantly ignored the inquiry and followed through with his plan (v. 4).

B. Specifically. First Chronicles 21 gives us deeper insight into what motivated David to take the census.

> Then Satan stood up against Israel and moved David to number Israel. (v. 1)

Somehow, Satan found an opening into David's mind—a crack in his character that pride had created—and moved him to place his confidence in manpower instead of in God. After counseling David against his plan (v. 3), Joab took the census and brought David the results.

147

> And Joab gave the number of the census of all the people to David. And all Israel were 1,100,000 men who drew the sword; and Judah was 470,000 men who drew the sword. (v. 5)

But the census was incomplete. Disturbed by David's command, Joab refused to number the men of Benjamin and Levi (v. 6).

C. Personally. David's decision reveals two things about his personal life. First, *he was out of touch with the Lord.* We don't read of prayer, of seeking God's counsel, of searching God's Word for help in his decision. He simply decided to do it. Second, *he was unaccountable to anyone around him.* Having reached a peerless position as the king of Israel, David answered to nobody.

Life on the Pedestal

If you find yourself in the trusted position of unquestioned authority, be careful. Life on the pedestal is precarious. When you fall from the heights, you not only fall hard, you shatter the lives of those beneath you. Don't live your life unchecked. Surround yourself with those who put integrity on a pedestal—not you.

II. Consequences of Disobedience

David paid a dear price for his foolish decision—he sacrificed his peace on pride's altar.

> Now David's heart troubled him after he had numbered the people. (2 Sam. 24:10a)

In Hebrew, *troubled* means "to be stricken, attacked, assaulted, crippled, destroyed." His heart crushed under the heels of guilt, David admitted his wrong before God.

> So David said to the Lord, "I have sinned greatly in what I have done. But now, O Lord, please take away the iniquity of Thy servant, for I have acted very foolishly." (v. 10b)

A. A choice to make. Instead of issuing David's punishment Himself, God made David choose his own consequences—perhaps the most severe punishment of all.

> And the Lord spoke to Gad, David's seer, saying, "Go and speak to David, saying, 'Thus says the Lord, "I offer you three things; choose for yourself one of them, that I may do it to you." ' " So Gad came to David and said to him, "Thus says the Lord, 'Take for yourself either three years of famine, or three months to be swept away before your foes, while the sword

of your enemies overtakes you, or else three days of
the sword of the Lord, even pestilence in the land,
and the angel of the Lord destroying throughout all
the territory of Israel.' Now, therefore, consider what
answer I shall return to Him who sent me." (1 Chron.
21:9–12)

B. Guilt to endure. Faced with the grim ramifications of this
choice, David was overwhelmed by guilt.

And David said to Gad, "I am in great distress."[1] (v. 13a)

But, repentantly, he chose the third consequence, falling into
God's hand rather than being given to the merciless hand of
man (v. 13b).

C. Confession to declare. As a result of David's sin, seventy
thousand Israelites died by an angel's sword (vv. 14–15). When
David saw the angel wielding its sword over Jerusalem, he fell
on his face and begged God to spare His people, claiming full
responsibility for his sin.

And David said to God, "Is it not I who commanded
to count the people? Indeed, I am the one who has
sinned and done very wickedly, but these sheep, what
have they done? O Lord my God, please let Thy hand
be against me and my father's household, but not
against Thy people that they should be plagued."
(v. 17)

The Shepherd's Responsibility

In the New Testament, James warns us about the responsibility leaders have to their flocks:

Let not many of you become teachers, my
brethren, knowing that as such we shall incur
a stricter judgment. (3:1)

Why does God judge shepherds more stringently than
sheep? Because they have the authority to either lead the
sheep to the still waters or into a pack of wolves.

Leaders, take your spiritual life seriously. You won't
bear the consequences alone. If you play games with sin,
innocent lambs will get hurt.

III. Altar and Deliverance

A. Command and obedience. God wanted David to build a
monument . . . an altar that would end the plague and stand as
a never-to-be-forgotten memory of this event.

---

1. In Hebrew, *distress* means a condition of being "tied up, restricted, cramped."

Then the angel of the Lord commanded Gad to say
to David, that David should go up and build an altar
to the Lord on the threshing floor of Ornan[2] the
Jebusite. (1 Chron. 21:18)

The consequences of disobedience fresh in his mind, David readily obeyed.

B. **Offer and response.** When Ornan saw David coming, he ran to him, bowed his face before him, and, full of respect, asked him:

"Why has my lord the king come to his servant?" And
David said, "To buy the threshing floor from you, in
order to build an altar to the Lord, that the plague
may be held back from the people." (2 Sam. 24:21)

Ornan generously offered to give David not only the threshing floor but also

"the oxen for the burnt offering, the threshing sledges
and the yokes of the oxen for the wood. Everything,
O king, [Ornan] gives to the king." (vv. 22b–23a)

And for free. But David refused to take the threshing floor without paying for it. In David's words,

"I will surely buy it from you for a price, for I will not
offer burnt offerings to the Lord my God which cost
me nothing." (v. 24b)

C. **Construction and relief.** When David built the altar, God responded graciously (v. 25).

And the Lord commanded the angel, and he put his
sword back in its sheath. (1 Chron. 21:27)

The Lord ended the plague, but because of David's foolish choice there were still seventy thousand fresh graves in Israel.

IV. Three Practical Suggestions

As we have seen through this sobering chapter in David's life, nobody—no matter how old, how wise, how respected—is immune to sin. But there are some things we can do to keep from making foolish decisions that damage our lives and those around us.

A. **Be accountable.** To live an unaccountable life is to invite danger.

B. **Remember sin's consequences.** Keep the seventy thousand Israelite graves fresh in your mind.

C. **Take God seriously.** Failing to do so is to deny His lordship in our lives. It's true. We will never outgrow sin altogether, but by His grace, we can learn to hate it more deeply . . . to see it less frequently in our lives.

---

2. Referred to as Araunah in 2 Samuel 24.

Living Insights

The Bible never flatters its heroes. Scripture is always true to life, right down to feet of clay. This study has allowed us to see David in both wise moments and foolish.

● Can you name a weakness or flaw in the following people? If you can't recall any problems, check out their stories in Scripture. Remember, the purpose of this exercise is not to put down men of the Bible, but rather to remember their humanity—that they struggled as we do today. Use this as a time to reflect on God's grace in your life.

People	Problems
Noah	
Abraham	
Moses	
Samson	
Solomon	
Jonah	
Peter	

Continued on next page

Living Insights

Why do the godly wander from spirituality? We suggested three reasons in this lesson: unaccountability, ignoring sin's consequences, and failing to take God seriously. Let's talk about them.

- Are you accountable? To whom? Does this accountability extend to all parts of your life? If you're unaccountable, why? What will it take to begin this process in your life?

- Can you recall times in your past when you have ignored sin's consequences? What was the outcome? With what sin do you battle? Have you considered the consequences? Think soberly on the effects it might have in your life.

- Failing to take God seriously is to deny His lordship. Do you agree with that statement? Why or why not? What is it that you've not yet surrendered to Christ? What keeps you from that full surrender? Share your thoughts with God in prayer.

The End of an Era
1 Chronicles 28–29

Some men mark the beginning of an era by forging new and uncharted courses, standing alone against the inevitable critics and enemies of change. Others mark the end of an era with their death. As they pass on, they leave a chasm that no one seems able to fill.

David—the man after God's own heart—was like that. Although his son Solomon was destined to become great, he was never really the man his father had been.

In Acts 13:36, we find a profound statement that underscores the significance of David's life.

> "For David, after he had *served the purpose of God in his own generation,* fell asleep, and was laid among his fathers." (emphasis added)

David had faithfully led Israel for forty years; fathered Solomon, God's chosen successor to the throne; and perpetuated the righteousness of Israel. And in 1 Chronicles 28–29, we see him in the final chapter of his life. Realizing he was near death—heart and mind swelling with emotion and memories—David reflected, advised his son, prayed, and rejoiced; his death ending an era that would never be duplicated in the annals of history.

I. Reflecting on the Temple: An Unfulfilled Desire
As David's life draws to a close, he calls together an assembly of all his national leaders, including his son Solomon, the king-elect, and reflects on an unfulfilled dream (1 Chron. 28:1–2).
A. His desire. His desire was simple . . . even pure. He had wanted to build a home for the sacred ark of the covenant.
> Then King David rose to his feet and said, "Listen to me, my brethren and my people; I had intended to build a permanent home for the ark of the covenant of the Lord and for the footstool of our God. So I had made preparations to build it." (v. 2)

B. God's answer. But God told David no.
> "But God said to me, 'You shall not build a house for My name because you are a man of war and have shed blood.' " (v. 3)

Although the cherished ambition to build a temple was born in David, it was to be carried out by Solomon (v. 6).
C. His response. David accepted God's no without a trace of bitterness or resentment.
> "Yet, the Lord, the God of Israel, chose me from all the house of my father to be king over Israel forever.

For He has chosen Judah to be a leader; and in the
house of Judah, my father's house, and among the
sons of my father He took pleasure in me to make
me king over all Israel." (v. 4)

Rather than pining the last few years of his life away with an
ache for that unfulfilled desire, David focuses on what the Lord
will allow him to do (vv. 5–8).

Unfulfilled Dreams

Has God said no to one of your dreams? Maybe a great
accomplishment . . . a certain career . . . a ministry . . . a relationship? If so, relinquish it. Let it go. Like David, focus
instead on what the Lord *will* do in your life. And be
thankful.

II. Speaking to His Son: An Untried Ruler

David turns to counsel Solomon—inexperienced, untried, un-
scarred—seeing in him the possibility of fulfilling his dream.

A. Regarding godliness. With his first piece of advice David
counsels his son on some of the fine points of godliness (v. 9a).

"As for you, my son Solomon, know the God of your
father."

1. **Know the Lord.** Understanding the difficulties of ruling a
nation, David counsels Solomon to know God. Philippians
3:10a beautifully describes what knowing God means:

[For my determined purpose is] that I may know
Him—that I may progressively become more
deeply and intimately acquainted with Him, per-
ceiving and recognizing and understanding [the
wonders of His Person] more strongly and more
clearly.[1] (brackets in original)

2. **Serve the Lord.** David tells Solomon to serve God in two
ways:

"And serve Him with a whole heart and a willing
mind; for the Lord searches all hearts, and under-
stands every intent of the thoughts." (1 Chron.
28:9b)

David—sweet singer of Israel—knows that God examines
His children's hearts and sees their every motive (Ps. 139:1–4,
23–24). So he urges Solomon to serve the Lord with a sincere
heart and a willing mind.

---

1. Amplified Bible, as quoted in *The Comparative Study Bible: A Parallel Bible* (Grand Rapids,
Mich.: Zondervan Bible Publishers, 1984).

3. Seek the Lord. David also urges his son to seek God, be sensitive to Him, listen to the nudgings of His voice.

> "If you seek Him, He will let you find Him; but if you forsake Him, He will reject you forever." (1 Chron. 28:9c)

Parent to Child

Parents, what kind of counsel do you most often give your children? "Clean up that room . . . I don't want you hanging around with him . . . finish your homework before you watch TV." Or is it "Know God . . . serve Him . . . seek Him"?

B. Regarding construction. Next, David unrolls the blueprints for the temple, explaining them room by room (vv. 11–19).

> "All this," said David, "the Lord made me understand in writing by His hand upon me, all the details of this pattern." (v. 19)

C. Regarding ruling. David knew that, as Israel's king, Solomon would often find himself in the pressure cooker, so he encouraged him with a reminder of God's faithfulness.

> Then David said to his son Solomon, "Be strong and courageous, and act; do not fear nor be dismayed, for the Lord God, my God, is with you. He will not fail you nor forsake you until all the work for the service of the house of the Lord is finished." (v. 20)

III. Praying from His Heart: An Unchanging Father

After counseling Solomon, David takes time to pray for his young son. Three things mark this prayer, one of the last David ever uttered.

A. Praise. David leaves man out of his prayer; his focus is unblurred and vertical, fixed on the majesty of God.

> So David blessed the Lord in the sight of all the assembly; and David said, "Blessed art Thou, O Lord God of Israel our father, forever and ever. Thine, O Lord, is the greatness and the power and the glory and the victory and the majesty, indeed everything that is in the heavens and the earth; Thine is the dominion, O Lord, and Thou dost exalt Thyself as head over all. Both riches and honor come from Thee, and Thou dost rule over all, and in Thy hand is power and might; and it lies in Thy hand to make great, and to strengthen everyone. Now therefore, our God, we thank Thee, and praise Thy glorious name." (29:10–13)

B. Thanksgiving. Verse 16 articulates the gratitude in David's heart:

> "O Lord our God, all this abundance that we have provided to build Thee a house for Thy holy name, it is from Thy hand, and all is Thine."

Though surrounded by riches, David never let them capture his heart.

C. Intercession. David concludes his prayer by asking God to touch the hearts of both the nation and his son.

> "O Lord, the God of Abraham, Isaac, and Israel, our fathers, preserve this forever in the intentions of the heart of Thy people, and direct their heart to Thee; and give to my son Solomon a perfect heart to keep Thy commandments, Thy testimonies, and Thy statutes, and to do them all, and to build the temple, for which I have made provision." (vv. 18–19)

IV. Rejoicing of the Assembly: An Undivided People

Finally, David turns to his people. Together, they bless the Lord . . . together they pay homage to the Lord and to the king (v. 20). Then, quietly, the Holy Spirit shines the light back on David; except now, David's lamp is dim—the candle of his life is about to go out.

> Then he died in a ripe old age, full of days, riches and honor. (v. 28a)

The End of Your Era

Like David, we all have a purpose for our lives. What has God given you to do in your generation?

God gifted David with political wisdom, strength, and, most importantly, a soft heart. How has He gifted you? When you die, will it be said that you fulfilled God's purpose for your life?

 Living Insights

Study One ▪▪▪▪▪▪▪▪▪▪▪▪▪▪▪▪▪▪▪▪▪▪▪▪▪▪▪▪

David . . . known to most only as the boy who killed Goliath. It is our hope that this series has filled in the gaps in your understanding of this man of God.

• Let's use our Living Insights today to reflect on the life we have studied. Page through the Scriptures and glance over the study guide in order to make entries in the following charts. Put a check by *truths* that you did not know before this series.

David's Strengths	
References	Observations

David's Weaknesses	
References	Observations

David's Relationship with God	
References	Observations

Continued on next page

David's Relationships with Others	
References	Observations

 Living Insights

Study Two ━━━━━━━━

We all have our favorites among the Bible characters. Often they're special because we can relate to their style. How about David? Could you relate to his life? Did you find personal application within giant-killing? Running from an enemy? Needing a hiding place? A situation of moral compromise? Family breakdown? Support from friends? The songs of praise?

● Using the following chart, make note of some key *applications* you have gained from this series. On the left, write out a principle or observation from David's life. Then jot down how this affects your life. How will you be different as a result of this series? It is our wish that we will all be more Christlike because of our time studying the life of David.

Truths from David's Life	Applications to My Life

Truths from David's Life	Applications to My Life

Books for Probing Further

David was paradox personified.

He slew Goliath with the fling of a stone, but he was wounded by the lust of his own wandering eyes. He soothed Saul's spirit with soft strains on the harp, but he exploded in anger at Nabal. He gave Jonathan's crippled son Mephibosheth grace—a seat at his royal table—but he ignored the needs of his own children. He hid from God after his affair with Bathsheba . . . but, oh, he knew how to draw near.

How can such an inconsistent man be considered someone after God's own heart? David's heart beat with God's not because he was perfect, but because he was *devoted.* One passion was greater than all the others: his desire to know and obey God.

We hope this study of David's life has compelled you to put your ears to God's Word and listen for His heartbeat—so that yours will begin to pulse to it. The following books will help you in your pursuit.

Bridges, Ronald F. *First Love.* Colorado Springs, Colo.: NavPress, 1987. Despite all his weaknesses, David was strong in his devotion and love for God. Is devotion to God one of your strong points too? Or is it a weak area that gets pushed back by the many demands on your time? With a warm, readable style, this book will challenge you to pursue your passion for God.

Foster, Richard J. *Celebration of Discipline: The Path to Spiritual Growth.* San Francisco, Calif.: Harper and Row, Publishers, 1978. Most of us think of discipline as anything but a celebration. Yet in this dynamic book, the author sheds the common sackcloth-and-ashes mentality toward spiritual discipline and urges us instead to maintain a deep joy while breaking free from the polarizing habits that distance us from God.

Inrig, Gary. *Quality Friendship.* Chicago, Ill.: Moody Press, 1981. The best example of biblical friendship is found in David's relationship with Jonathan. In this book, the author uses David and Jonathan to model the type of friendships all of us should build—friendships based on loyalty, commitment, and a deep love.

Keller, W. Phillip. *David: The Time of Saul's Tyranny.* Waco, Tex.: Word Books, 1985. *David: The Shepherd King.* Waco, Tex.: Word Books, 1986. In these two volumes, the author uniquely blends keen scholarship with a sensitive, devotional style. Familiarizing you with the life of this godly yet very human man, Keller paints these portraits of David's life with dramatic colors. Throughout this book, the author will confront you with the stark call to obedience.

Kreeft, Peter. *Making Sense Out of Suffering.* Ann Arbor, Mich.: Servant Books, 1986. Like David, all of us go through stormy times. But, while David knew his suffering was the result of his sin, our suffering often seems random, pointless, cruel. This is a book for empty, groaning hearts. It provides the satisfying, biblical answer to the question of why we suffer.

Smedes, Lewis B. *Forgive and Forget: Healing the Hurts We Don't Deserve.* San Francisco, Calif.: Harper and Row, Publishers, 1984. This book is a treatise on being free. It explains not only how you can be free but why you need to be free from the hurts that embitter and bind you. And Smedes's honest approach is liberating as well. He expects no perfection, induces no guilt. He only encourages us to take steps toward being forgivers. Smedes closes his book with these words, "If you are *trying* to forgive; even if you manage forgiving in fits and starts, if you forgive today, hate again tomorrow, and have to forgive again the day after, you are a forgiver. Most of us are amateurs, bungling duffers sometimes. So what? In this game nobody is an expert. We are all beginners."

Swindoll, Charles R. *Killing Giants, Pulling Thorns.* Portland, Oreg.: Multnomah Press, 1978. Like David, we all face giants. Challenging us in the silent battleground of our souls are the big things. Things that buffet, bluster, and defy domination. Dark things. Ominous shadows that blight, blacken, and blot out the Son. This book provides a biblically based discussion on how to face the giants that threaten your spiritual life. With its poignant practicality, it will help ease your struggle and renew your heart.

White, John. *Parents in Pain.* Downers Grove, Ill.: InterVarsity Press, 1979. If you found yourself relating to David in the midst of his domestic whirlwind, you'll find help in this book. Compassionately, the author discusses feelings of guilt, frustration, anger, and the sense of inadequacy that parents experience when their children wrestle with problems like alcoholism, homosexuality, and suicide. Rich in both counsel and comfort, this book will help calm the storm in your home.

Wilkes, Peter. *Overcoming Anger & Other Dragons of the Soul: Shaking Loose from Persistent Sins.* Downers Grove, Ill.: InterVarsity Press, 1987. Anger . . . lust . . . pride: "dragons of the soul." David knew them, deep in the dank dungeon of his heart. What about you? In this book, the author shows us how to loose ourselves from the shackles of those persistent sins that imprison us.

Notes

Notes

Notes

Notes

Notes

Notes

Notes

Notes

Notes

Notes

Insight for Living
Cassette Tapes
David... A Man After God's Own Heart

Perhaps the most popular Old Testament character, David is a study in contrasts: an unknown shepherd lad who became the king, a rugged warrior who wrote tender psalms, a strong leader who was weak at home, a man of God with a rebellious son. This series introduces you to the facts revealed in Scripture and how they relate directly to us today. No biography could be more timely. Although David is dead, his life still speaks.

			U.S.	Canada
DAV	**CS**	Cassette series—includes album cover	**$65.25**	**$83.00**
		Individual cassettes—include messages A and B	5.00	6.35

These prices are effective as of June 1988 and are subject to change without notice.

DAV 1-A: *God's Heart, God's Man, God's Ways*—1 Samuel 13:13–14, 16:1; Psalm 78:70–72
    B: *A Nobody, Nobody Noticed*—1 Samuel 16:1–13

DAV 2-A: *Soft Music for a Hard Heart*—1 Samuel 16:14–23
    B: *David and the Dwarf*—1 Samuel 17

DAV 3-A: *Aftermath of a Giant-Killing*—1 Samuel 17:55–18:9
    B: *Every Crutch Removed*—1 Samuel 18–21

DAV 4-A: *For Cave Dwellers Only*—1 Samuel 22:1–2, Selected Psalms
    B: *Life's Most Subtle Temptation*—1 Samuel 24

DAV 5-A: *What to Feed an Angry Man*—1 Samuel 25
    B: *Cloudy Days . . . Dark Nights*—1 Samuel 27

DAV 6-A: *Two Deaths: Analysis and Analogies*—1 Samuel 31
    B: *New King, New Throne, Same Lord*—2 Samuel 1–5

DAV 7-A: *David and the Ark*—2 Samuel 6
    B: *When God Says No*—2 Samuel 7

DAV 8-A: *Grace in a Barren Place*—2 Samuel 9
    B: *The Case of the Open Window Shade*—2 Samuel 11

DAV 9-A: *Confrontation!*—2 Samuel 12:1–14
    B: *Trouble at Home*—2 Samuel 12–18, Galatians 6:7–8a

DAV 10-A: *Riding Out the Storm*—2 Samuel 12:13–25
    B: *Friends in Need*—2 Samuel 15–19

DAV 11-A: *Being Big Enough to Forgive*—2 Samuel 16:5–13, 19:16–23
    B: *A Song of Triumph*—2 Samuel 22

DAV 12-A: *When the Godly Are Foolish*—2 Samuel 24, 1 Chronicles 21
    B: *The End of an Era*—1 Chronicles 28–29

How to Order by Mail

Ordering is easy and convenient. Simply mark on the order form whether you want the series or individual tapes. Tear out the order form and mail it with your payment to the appropriate address listed under "Ordering Information" at the front of this guide. We will process your order as promptly as we can.

United States orders: If you wish your order to be shipped first-class for faster delivery, please add 10 percent of the total order amount (not including California sales tax). Otherwise, please allow four to six weeks for delivery by fourth-class mail. We accept personal checks, money orders, Visa, and Master-Card in payment for materials. Unfortunately, we are unable to offer invoicing or COD orders.

Canadian orders: Please add 7 percent of your total order for first-class postage and allow approximately four weeks for delivery. For our listeners in British Columbia, a 6 percent sales tax must also be added to the total of all tape orders (not including postage). For further information, please contact our office at 1-800-663-7639. We accept personal checks, money orders, Visa, or MasterCard in payment for materials. Unfortunately, we are unable to offer invoicing or COD orders.

Overseas orders: If you live outside the United States or Canada, please allow six to ten weeks for delivery by surface mail. If you would like your order sent airmail, the delivery time may be reduced. Whether you choose surface or airmail delivery, postage costs must be added to the amount of purchase and included with your order. Please use the following chart to determine the correct postage. Due to fluctuating currency rates, we can accept only personal checks made payable in U.S. funds, international money orders, Visa, or MasterCard in payment for materials.

Type of Postage	Cassettes
Surface	10% of total order
Airmail	25% of total order

For Faster Service, Order by Telephone

To purchase using Visa or MasterCard, you are welcome to use our **toll-free** numbers between the hours of 8:30 A.M. and 4:00 P.M., Pacific time, Monday through Friday. The number to call from anywhere in the United States is **1-800-772-8888.** To order from Canada, call 1-800-663-7639. Telephone orders from overseas are handled through our Sales Department at (714) 870-9161. We are unable to accept collect calls.

Our Guarantee

Our cassettes are guaranteed for ninety days against faulty performance or breakage due to a defect in the tape. For best results, please be sure your tape recorder is in good operating condition and is cleaned regularly.

Note: To cover processing and handling, there is a $10 fee for *any* returned check.

Order Form

Please send me the following cassette tapes:

The current series: ☐ DAV CS David . . . A Man After God's Own Heart

Individual tapes:
☐ DAV 1   ☐ DAV 4   ☐ DAV 7   ☐ DAV 10
☐ DAV 2   ☐ DAV 5   ☐ DAV 8   ☐ DAV 11
☐ DAV 3   ☐ DAV 6   ☐ DAV 9   ☐ DAV 12

I am enclosing:

$ _____ To purchase the cassette series for $65.25 (in Canada $83.00*) which includes the album cover

$ _____ To purchase individual tapes at $5.00 each (in Canada $6.35*)

$ _____ Total of purchases

$ _____ If the order will be delivered in California, please add 6 percent sales tax

$ _____ U.S. residents please add 10 percent for first-class shipping and handling if desired

$ _____ *British Columbia residents please add 6 percent sales tax

$ _____ Canadian residents please add 7 percent for postage

$ _____ **Overseas residents please add appropriate postage** (See postage chart under "How to Order by Mail.")

$ _____ As a gift to the Insight for Living radio ministry for which a tax-deductible receipt will be issued

$ _____ **Total amount due (Please do not send cash.)**

Form of payment:

☐ Check or money order made payable to Insight for Living

☐ Credit card (Visa or MasterCard only)

If there is a balance: ☐ apply it as a donation   ☐ please refund

---

Credit card purchases:

☐ Visa   ☐ MasterCard Number _____

Expiration Date _____

Signature _____

We cannot process your credit card purchase without your signature.

Name _____

Address _____

_____

City _____

State/Province _____ Zip/Postal Code _____

Country _____

Telephone (_____) _____ Radio Station __ __ __ __

Should questions arise concerning your order, we may need to contact you.

Order Form

Please send me the following cassette tapes:

The current series: ☐ DAV CS David . . . A Man After God's Own Heart

Individual tapes:
☐ DAV 1 ☐ DAV 4 ☐ DAV 7 ☐ DAV 10
☐ DAV 2 ☐ DAV 5 ☐ DAV 8 ☐ DAV 11
☐ DAV 3 ☐ DAV 6 ☐ DAV 9 ☐ DAV 12

I am enclosing:

$ _____ To purchase the cassette series for $65.25 (in Canada $83.00*) which includes the album cover

$ _____ To purchase individual tapes at $5.00 each (in Canada $6.35*)

$ _____ Total of purchases

$ _____ If the order will be delivered in California, please add 6 percent sales tax

$ _____ U.S. residents please add 10 percent for first-class shipping and handling if desired

$ _____ *British Columbia residents please add 6 percent sales tax

$ _____ Canadian residents please add 7 percent for postage

$ _____ **Overseas residents please add appropriate postage** (See postage chart under "How to Order by Mail.")

$ _____ As a gift to the Insight for Living radio ministry for which a tax-deductible receipt will be issued

$ _____ **Total amount due (Please do not send cash.)**

Form of payment:

☐ Check or money order made payable to Insight for Living

☐ Credit card (Visa or MasterCard only)

If there is a balance: ☐ apply it as a donation ☐ please refund

---

Credit card purchases:

☐ Visa ☐ MasterCard Number _____

Expiration Date _____

Signature _____

We cannot process your credit card purchase without your signature.

Name _____

Address _____

_____

City _____

State/Province _____ Zip/Postal Code _____

Country _____

Telephone ( ) _____ Radio Station __ __ __ __

Should questions arise concerning your order, we may need to contact you.

Order Form

Please send me the following cassette tapes:

The current series: ☐ DAV CS David ... A Man After God's Own Heart

Individual tapes:
☐ DAV 1   ☐ DAV 4   ☐ DAV 7   ☐ DAV 10
☐ DAV 2   ☐ DAV 5   ☐ DAV 8   ☐ DAV 11
☐ DAV 3   ☐ DAV 6   ☐ DAV 9   ☐ DAV 12

I am enclosing:

$ _____ To purchase the cassette series for $65.25 (in Canada $83.00*) which includes the album cover

$ _____ To purchase individual tapes at $5.00 each (in Canada $6.35*)

$ _____ Total of purchases

$ _____ If the order will be delivered in California, please add 6 percent sales tax

$ _____ U.S. residents please add 10 percent for first-class shipping and handling if desired

$ _____ *British Columbia residents please add 6 percent sales tax

$ _____ Canadian residents please add 7 percent for postage

$ _____ **Overseas residents please add appropriate postage** (See postage chart under "How to Order by Mail.")

$ _____ As a gift to the Insight for Living radio ministry for which a tax-deductible receipt will be issued

$ _____ **Total amount due (Please do not send cash.)**

Form of payment:

☐ Check or money order made payable to Insight for Living
☐ Credit card (Visa or MasterCard only)
If there is a balance: ☐ apply it as a donation   ☐ please refund

---

Credit card purchases:

☐ Visa   ☐ MasterCard Number _____

Expiration Date _____

Signature _____

We cannot process your credit card purchase without your signature.

Name _____

Address _____

_____

City _____

State/Province _____ Zip/Postal Code _____

Country _____

Telephone ( ) _____ Radio Station __ __ __ __

Should questions arise concerning your order, we may need to contact you.